BIPOLAR DISORDER THROUGH MY EYES

A MEMOIR OF HOPE

BIPOLAR DISORDER THROUGH MY EYES

DAVID WILLIAM WEISNER

Copyright © 2024 David William Weisner

All rights reserved. No part of this publication in print or in electronic format may be reproduced, stored in a retrieval system, or transmitted in any form or by any means, electronic, mechanical, photocopying, recording, or otherwise without the prior written permission of the publisher.

The scanning, uploading, and distribution of this book without permission is a theft of the author's intellectual property. Thank you for your support of the author's rights.

Editing, design, distribution by Bublish

ISBN: 978-1-647048-63-1 (paperback)
ISBN: 978-1-647048-65-5 (eBook)

For Mom

CONTENTS

Introduction ix
Chapter 1: Prudence 1
Chapter 2: Two Years Homeless In Los Angeles . . 10
Chapter 3: Albuquerque, New Mexico . . . 22
Chapter 4: Childhood 26
Chapter 5: Camp Cejwin 35
Chapter 6: High School 41
Chapter 7: Butch 53
Chapter 8: LSD 58
Chapter 9: State University Of New York At Buffalo . 64
Chapter 10: Manic Flight To Florida 72
Chapter 11: Marlboro Psychiatric Hospital . . . 79
Chapter 12: Men Get Molested Too 84
Chapter 13: New Paltz, New York 90
Chapter 14: Olivia 100

Chapter 15: Erin 109
Chapter 16: Susan 117
Chapter 17: Maria 132
Chapter 18: Learning Guitar 139
Chapter 19: Depressive Episode 147
Chapter 20: Rikers Island 154
Chapter 21: After Rikers 164
Chapter 22: Living In Staten Island Again . . .172
Chapter 23: Living In Stone Ridge, New York . . .183
Chapter 24: Living In Woodstock, New York . . . 191
Chapter 25: Living In Monroe Township, New Jersey .199
Epilogue 209

INTRODUCTION

This memoir is the true story of my life as a man afflicted with bipolar disorder. I write this now as a person who has been very stable and happy for the last ten years, but I will take you back into the tempest that was a good portion of my adult life. I have suffered through many things, including manic highs, suicidal lows, and, in my younger years, drug and alcohol abuse.

I have spent years homeless, having to beg for food or eat out of garbage cans. I have been locked up countless times in mental hospitals or in jail. I have spent months in some of the worst jails in the United States, including a year in New York City's notorious jail complex known as Rikers Island.

Between these extremely low and difficult points, I have had many good years as well, when I was properly stable on the right medications. During those good years, I was able to get a college degree in sociology, and I experienced many great times.

I taught myself how to play the piano at the age of five, and in my twenties, I studied classical guitar with a gifted teacher who became my mentor. It was this that allowed me the honor of teaching many students in guitar and piano, which I did when I was stable enough to work.

In my thirties, I wrote freelance and published many magazine articles about spirituality. I also published some poetry and even got paid for it.

When I was stable, I was able to help many people, especially the elderly, in dealing with life and their problems. I worked at a senior residence where I acted as a counselor for many who just needed someone to talk to.

I have had great love affairs throughout my life and have been lucky enough to know some amazing women. In addition, I have had many friends along the way and have lived, laughed, and experienced so many happy times as well.

Throughout it all my family has stood by me, always being a pillar of strength, support, and love. We all need a robust support system, and my family—especially my mother—has been the reason I survived and am now thriving so well. I don't think it is an exaggeration to say that without my mom's love, support, and intervention over the years, I would surely have been long dead by now.

I have also been on a spiritual quest all my life. I studied for many years with a Buddhist monk, learning meditation and philosophy. I learned some of the ancient arts from shamans and reiki masters. This is in addition to the thousands of books I have read on such topics as the religions of the world and major philosophies.

I believe my greatest knowledge has come from prayer and observation of the natural world. I have spent countless hours in prayer and out in nature learning so much that even books could not tell.

What I have discovered at the age of fifty-four is my own slant on God and religion. Even though I was born Jewish, I don't practice any particular religion. Instead, I follow what I have perceived as the right way to live. I believe in reincarnation and karma, and I believe in the maxim of "Do unto others as you would like to be done unto you."

I think that being a good person is the most important thing in the world and that kindness is all that matters in the end. In my way of looking at things, I believe with all my heart that life is a school and God is the teacher. I believe we have been put here to learn and to become more enlightened and empathetic souls.

When we die, we go to heaven, where we reassess how we did in the classroom of life, and then we eventually come back to learn more lessons. I believe in a loving and just God.

To that end, I believe the very difficult life I have lived was a gift from God so that I would become a better soul and be able to help others who struggle along a similar path. What I know for sure is that we are all God's children. There is no difference between a Jew or a Muslim or a Hindu or a Christian. We are all the children of God, our father, and we all go to heaven when we die. As I said, this life is just a learning experience. It's what I like to call the little blue schoolhouse.

It does not matter if we are Black or white or Asian or woman or man; we are like an actor playing different roles in different lives. These physical differences are essentially an illusion and that is why it is so distressing and ignorant that we hate anyone based on this illusion. We should love everyone as God loves all of us as his children. We are one family for real.

As you will discover in this memoir, I have not presented it in chronological order but instead use flashbacks or sometimes jump ahead in the chapters to tell my story. I have even included some chapters on specific people, places, or events that have been important in my life. I have also changed everyone's name to preserve their privacy.

I sincerely wish that you get something from this book, and that is the gift of hope. We all have our crosses to bear, and there is always someone who has had more troubles or a more difficult life, but I have learned through my struggles to be grateful for everything I have now. From someone like me, who has literally lost everything at different points, I no longer take anything for granted. I realize it's the simple things in life that are important. If you have a roof over your head and food and family and love and some friends, you are a very rich person.

This life is not easy for anyone. We all go through hard times, but if you have a little courage, a lot of faith in God, and love and forgiveness in your heart, you can get through anything.

Chapter 1

PRUDENCE

(2004)

I had been working part time at Island Shores Senior Residence on Staten Island as a recreational aide and was very stable on different meds. It was during this time that I met a woman online called Prudence. It was not a love connection, as she had a boyfriend and I was not attracted to her in a romantic fashion. She was extremely overweight and a few years older than me. After a good amount of chatting online, we realized that her former mother-in-law was a patient at the senior residence and that I knew her very well. We decided that we would meet there when she came to visit her mother-in-law.

Prudence arrived with her boyfriend and three children. She was a very colorful woman. She liked to wear bright dresses and lots of new age jewelry. We hit it off right away, and it seemed like I was going to make a new friend. Little did I realize how important this woman and her family would become to me over the next ten years.

She invited me over for dinner one night, and I had a great time. She is Italian and an amazing cook, and Italian food is my favorite. Prudence was a gracious host, and her boyfriend and three daughters were wonderful people as well. It was not long before I became a frequent visitor to her house. Eventually I was spending every Christmas and New Years with her, and I was over there about three to four times per week. Prudence had become my best friend.

We had so much in common, and we loved to talk for hours. She was very spiritual, as I am, and we discussed past lives and reincarnation and religion and philosophy. She also loved nature and animals, as I do. At some point she found five abandoned newborn kittens in her backyard. She took them in and nursed them as her own, getting up every two hours to feed them formula from a dropper. The kittens were so adorable, and their eyes were not even open yet.

Unfortunately, one of the kittens was too small and died very soon, but the others grew up to be strong, beautiful cats and lived many years with her and her family. She was very nurturing and had that earth mother vibe going on.

My dating life was not going well at that point, and Prudence tried to set me up with different people. One was with a woman she knew from online who lived in Brooklyn, which turned into a total nightmare date, and another was with a beautiful blonde who taught at her daughter's Catholic school.

The date went very well. We hung out at the Muddy Cup coffee shop and listened to music. The teacher kept referencing our next date together and was very flirty, but she would not let me kiss her good night. Eventually it got back to me that she only wanted to date a Catholic guy. I was upset because I really liked her and we had gotten along so well.

Prudence's boyfriend, Gary, who by now was her husband, was a doorman and worked in the city. He suffered from fibromyalgia, a very disabling disease that caused him great pain. He took medicine for it, but I think he was always tired and achy. Gary and I got along very well; he was an artist and a writer. Prudence told me sometimes that he was jealous of our relationship, but I knew that was silly because we were strictly platonic. Gary might have been envious of how much time we spent together, though, which was understandable. Gary and her ex-husband weren't on the greatest of terms, and they even had a violent fistfight in the living room one day.

Prudence was always putting down her ex to me and in front of the kids, which I did not approve of. He really was not a bad guy, but she seemed to despise him. It was his money, though, that kept the family above water, as he had a very good job as a building engineer and really loved his children. Prudence worked part time as a saleswoman at Sears.

Prudence and I liked to hang out at the wonderful parks on Staten Island and look at the water or go for walks. Sometimes we and the family would go out to dinner, and Prudence seemed to always complain to the staff about something, which could be very embarrassing.

After many years of great friendship, I was comfortably one of the family. Her oldest daughter, Lily, and I had become very close. Sometimes after dinner, Lily, who was now nineteen, and I would go for a drive and sit at the park watching the water. We had long in-depth conversations and usually laughed and laughed.

Lily was curvy and had stunning hazel eyes and was nothing but beautiful to me. She was great with fashion and hair and was in beauty school, on her way to becoming a hairdresser.

Over the time period we were hanging out, I grew more and more fond of Lily, and I developed a huge crush on her. We had so many things in common. She was an artist and loved to sing, and she had some of her paintings tattooed on her arms. We talked on the phone a lot, and I loved her sense of humor. She introduced to me much of the new music coming out, like Lady Gaga, and I started listening to modern pop music instead of just the classic rock I had enjoyed for years.

When I was forty and she was twenty, I started to fall madly in love with her, but I knew it could never be because her mother was my best friend in the world. My mother even had a dream that I hooked up with Lily and that it completely destroyed everything in my life. I knew I could never be with her, but this dream proved to be prophetic.

It was about that time that my psychiatrist decided to take me off my medicine. He said he had a "pet theory" that when people reach their forties and fifties, bipolar disorder kind of burns itself out, and I could stop taking my medication. Even though I'd been perfectly stable for many years and was working two jobs, one teaching piano and guitar privately and the other teaching piano two days a week at Staten Island Music School, he wanted me to be free of meds.

Over the next few months, I started to unravel. My shaman teacher had also supported me coming off the meds, as she thought that with all the work we had done together, I was healed of bipolar disorder and would not need them anymore. I trusted these two people completely, but what a price I would pay for not staying on my meds. My good life was about to be turned completely upside down.

One night Lily and I went to my friend's art gallery opening, and we took pictures and posted them on Facebook. My shaman teacher saw the pictures and told me that she observed a purple cord between my heart and Lily's heart and that to her it indicated we were "twin flames" and were meant to be together. I was off my medication and not seeing the world clearly anymore, so I listened to my shaman teacher and felt that Lily must be my soulmate. I was so deeply in love with her.

One night we were hanging out at my apartment and talking on the couch when I simply took her hand in mine. We held hands for over two hours and never said a word to each other. It was such a beautiful moment, and I wanted to hold her hand forever. At about four in the morning, she said she probably should go, and I drove her home.

At this point I felt that Lily and I were drawing closer and that it was inevitable we would end up together. If I'd been on my medicine, I know this would never have happened. I would have been completely rational and would have never ruined my relationship with Lily's mother. Prudence invited me to her house for dinner as usual, and I prepared to go. When I got outside to my car, I noticed a tire was flat, which I perceived as a message from the angels to stop immediately. I ignored it, and my mother let me use her car instead. At Prudence's house that evening, a strong intuition came over me, and I knew we would never have dinner together again. I realized my fate was now sealed.

Lily and I left after dinner and went to the music studio at my apartment. After playing some music and talking for hours, we went to my bedroom. I told her I thought she would be the perfect girlfriend. She agreed but said we couldn't be together because of my friendship with her mother. I concurred, and for a few moments, I was relieved because I knew pursuing something with Lily would lead to my destruction. I laid on my bed, and she sat in my office chair, and we continued to talk.

A few moments later, she confessed her love for me. She told me that since we first met at the senior residence ten years before, she had been completely and hopelessly in love with me and had never stopped thinking about me. She prayed that we would end up together one day.

I sat up in bed and reached for the arms of the office chair she was sitting in. I pulled her close to me and kissed her perfect lips. We started making out, and it was amazingly beautiful. In my mind I kept thinking, *I can't believe this is really happening!*

We kissed and cuddled for hours. I was in heaven. I never thought it would be possible, but at long last, I was together with the woman I loved.

We decided that we would tell Prudence soon and hoped that she would accept it. We expressed our love for each other again and again. We were both so happy. I drove her home, and we kissed goodbye around the block from her house. We were so thankful that we had admitted our love for each other and were eager to begin our life together and date openly.

Lily called the next day. She had already told her mother about us. Prudence was flipping out; I could hear her screaming in the background.

Her mother wanted to know if she'd fucked me, and Lily kept telling her we had only kissed. To this, she screamed at her even more.

Gary took the phone to talk to me. I told him that Lily and I were soulmates, like he and Prudence. I told him that we were deeply in love and were planning to date. Gary said it didn't matter that I loved her; I needed to be the adult and not pursue this course of action.

By the next day, all hell was breaking loose in our worlds. Prudence was in full freak-out mode and told Lily that we had betrayed her and that she must choose between her mother or me. Lily chose me and was immediately thrown out of the house. Lily asked if she and her cat could move in with me. I knew that if I didn't say yes, I would lose her, so I agreed. It was not the situation I wanted or was prepared for. I thought we would be able to date like normal people, with her family's blessing, but apparently, I was dead wrong.

Lily told me I had to pick her up right then because her mother was throwing out all her stuff, including her paintings. I started the twenty-minute drive to their house, and Lily texted me the whole time that Gary was coming home from work and was going to punch me in the face. Gary is a big dude, at least six foot three and strong, so I was not happy about this prospect.

When I arrived, it was pure bedlam. Lily told me to wait in the car. Prudence was screaming at the top of her lungs, and Lily kept coming out with big black garbage bags of her stuff that she threw into my back seat and trunk. She tried to put her cat in the carrier, but he was freaking out too, and she couldn't get him in. I texted her to drop him in on his ass so that he couldn't get away. She did but not without getting scratched up.

When she came out to the car, her face was scratched, her hair and makeup were a huge mess, and she was sweating profusely and was utterly exhausted. Gary was not home yet, so we sped away. That was how Lily came to live with me.

We introduced her cat to my two cats slowly and kept them separate for a couple of days until they got used to one another's smell. Eventually they got along and learned to love one another, so that aspect of the move was not a problem. I was living in a two-bedroom apartment in the downstairs of my parents' house, and I used one of the bedrooms for my music studio.

Lily and I settled in. We got along great, but she and I were very stressed out by Prudence's actions. She went on the warpath for real, writing hateful emails to me and to Lily and to my mother and my shaman teacher and to all of Lily's friends. She tried to drive a wedge between us and them. She succeeded in turning some of Lily's best friends against her, and they wouldn't talk to her anymore. My mother, who was in Florida for the winter, was not happy either.

I was completely off my medications for bipolar disorder, and I was not thinking rationally. I had trouble sleeping, and my mind was racing. Lily and I were extremely upset. Prudence tried to cut Lily off from her two younger sisters, which was distressing to us both.

We had wonderful times together, though, and sometimes spent the whole night laughing. We fooled around but didn't go all the way for eleven days. When we did, it was the most beautiful experience of our lives. Sex with Lily was a completely spiritual. We loved each other so much that it was absolutely magical.

Lily gave me a haircut, but it did not come out that great. The second time she tried it, though, she completely nailed it. She showed me how to use products to keep it curly and full. We went out a lot and had a lot of fun. Lily even got me to go to the movies, which I hated doing, but we had a good time, even though we ran into some of her former friends.

Lily got another tattoo, but it got infected, so I called my cousin, who is a doctor, and she prescribed an antibiotic. When she moved in, Lily was working at Sears with Prudence, but her mother caused her such duress at the job that she had to quit. Prudence called her all kinds of names and talked about her to the bosses and her coworkers, making her work environment toxic and impossible to sustain. Now Lily had no job, and I was working only part time, so money was getting tight.

It did not help that Lily was constantly wanting me to buy her things and to go out to dinner and coffee frequently. At the time I had great credit and money in the bank but that would soon change for the worst. I tried to explain to Lily about money and finances, but she just got upset. She started to bother me at my job at the music school and kept calling me with her problems and fears. We argued over cooking and laundry. Prudence had done everything for her, and Lily was not prepared to live like an adult. When I accidentally left her shirt in the laundry overnight and it began to smell like mildew, she freaked out and we argued. Then I screamed at her to do it herself.

Lily needed a job to contribute to the household, so I lined up an interview for her at an art store. The day of the interview, she woke up with great pain in her abdomen and was crying. Understandably I was very concerned about it, but I asked if she could possibly go to the interview first and then I would take her straight to the hospital. She agreed, and I was so proud of her for showing such courage. She got the job, and we immediately went to the emergency room.

They gave her a battery of tests, including a sonogram, CT-scan, and pelvic exam, among others. They could not find anything wrong, so they give her pain medicine and sent her home. Later that night I asked if I could try to relax her by giving her Reiki. I am a trained Reiki practitioner, and in the past, I have been able to help people with pain management. She laid on her back on the bed, and I gave her a treatment with my hands. Within seconds her pain went completely away and never returned.

One night Lily's real father came for dinner. He was very supportive and knew how much we were in love and how much I tried to take care of his daughter. The age difference was not a factor for him. He was a good man and on our side.

Lily had been living with me over two months, but things were very tense despite our great love and affection for each other. She was isolated from most of her family now, and she wanted us to have children immediately. I was very against this and told her she was too young—maybe in the future we would have kids. In addition, there were problems with our eating habits. Because I was not on my meds, I could diet and was seeing a nutritionist and losing a ton of weight. I wanted to her to diet with me for her health but that caused problems.

We were stressed out, and Lily had multiple meltdowns. I was going into debt to support her and her lifestyle, and Lily and I realized that it was not working out. There was just too much stress, and she missed her sisters greatly. Lily moved into her father's apartment in a different part of Staten Island. I was in a state of manic psychosis after being off my medications for so long and having the horrible heartbreak of losing Prudence, Lily, and the whole family as my best friends. It turned into an unbelievable nightmare.

I ended up quitting the jobs I loved, teaching students privately and at the music school, and decided to move upstate to my favorite place on earth at the time, New Paltz. In an act of desperation and insanity, I sold or gave to the library more than a thousand books from my precious collection. I moved to New Paltz with only a few dollars, but I could not find a job, and soon I became homeless.

Chapter 2

TWO YEARS HOMELESS IN LOS ANGELES

(2011)

Being homeless in New Paltz was not so bad. I had the twenty-four-hour Laundromat to sleep in and the family of New Paltz food bank to keep me fed. At that time, I wanted to be near the music industry, so I decided to move to Los Angelos.

I had an old checkbook of my father's, and I used it to cash out $5,000. I would need that money to get an apartment and start a life in Los Angeles. I hated to leave my beloved New Paltz, but I could not fulfill my dreams while I stayed there.

I flew to Los Angeles and went to a small motel in Hollywood that was about a hundred bucks a night. The first night I went to Girls, Girls, Girls, a strip club nearby. I was drinking and having a great time with different strippers. At one point I was in the back room with three beautiful girls when I felt an intuition that one of them was going through my pants pocket for money. My pants were not on at the time, but I could sense it anyway. I was drunk and plenty delusional, so I thought she would just give me the money back or come home with me or whatever.

Unfortunately, I was being robbed, and when I got dressed to leave, she had cleaned me out of thousands and had left me with about seventy dollars. There I was in Los Angeles, trying to start my new life, and now I was homeless and penniless again.

I stayed in Hollywood for a few days. I went to the grocery store and pretended to shop while I ate my meals from the shelves. I tried to earn some money busking with my guitar, but I didn't have the patience for this and made very little. Eventually I made my way to Venice Beach, which is kind of a hippie town.

I slept on the beach and ate from a food bank stand during the day that was on the boardwalk. Some nights were cold, and once I had to cover my body with sand to stay warm. During the evening, I liked to hang out at Danny's, a popular bar and restaurant with nightly bands and entertainment. There they gave me water, and sometimes I ate people's leftovers when they were finished. Danny's was a great scene, and I used the bathroom sinks there every day to shower and wash my hair.

From a spa I stole some sneakers for my now bare feet and took a towel for a blanket to use at night. Venice was a great place to hang during the day, but at night it changed and could become very dangerous. On the beach covered with my towel, I watched the stars and felt completely alone in the universe. It was beautiful but ultimately very sad. I prayed before every meal and thanked God I was still alive. My life was completely fucked up, but I still had my dreams and my faith in God.

During the day I had to beg for money, which was humiliating. I hated it, but it was the only way to survive. I asked people for cigarettes as well and sometimes got them. I asked at the boardwalk pizzeria for a free slice, but they wouldn't give it to me. I was upset because pizza is my favorite food, and I couldn't even afford one slice. On the beach one day, a young man approached me and said, "Do you like cigarettes?"

"Yes!" I exclaimed joyfully.

"Regular or menthol?" he asked.

I told him menthol, and he gave me a whole pack. I was so happy that I gave him a huge hug and thanked him so much. It's amazing how much you can appreciate the little things when you have absolutely nothing in the world. I am much more thankful today for everything I have because of what I have been through.

Around three o'clock that morning, I was awakened by something. I looked up to see a man with a large knife in his hand, running along the beach toward me in a zigzag fashion. I knew he'd seen me and was coming directly at me. I grabbed the empty vodka bottle that I kept with me sometimes for protection. I held it out in front of me and knew that hitting him in the head would be the only way to stop him from stabbing me to death. Just then a miracle happened, and I knew I had a guardian angel for real that day. A strange force took my hand and banged the vodka bottle against the rocks, leaving it in a perfect broken shard. It was at that moment that the man approached me with his knife in the air, but when he saw the weapon I had, he stopped his attack and ran away.

If he had killed me that night, I would have been just another dead homeless person with no ID, and my parents, family, and friends would never know what had happened to me. I would have been missing forever from all the people who loved me.

On a far happier day, one morning I was walking close to the handball courts near Muscle Beach when I came upon an attractive woman in her thirties sleeping on the court. She seemed to have some sort of rash on her face. I talked to her, and we hung out that day. She brought me to a storage facility and gave me a jacket, a pair of sneakers, and some clothes. This kindhearted homeless woman paid for me to get a haircut and some cigarettes, and we went to a place that fed us for lunch one day. She was so very kind to me, and I was glad to have found a friend.

We hung out for a few days, and I was so happy to have someone who seemed to care. She looked out for me and tried to help in any way she could with her limited resources.

After spending a few days with this cool homeless person, I was left to my own devices again. A big problem came when the food bank on the boardwalk did not show up for a couple of days. I was extremely hungry and angry. I didn't know what to do. I begged for change, but no one was helping me, and I was in a panic. Do you know what it's like to be truly hungry and have no one to help you or to have no food or money in sight?

In my desperate state, I walked into a restaurant and sat down at a barstool. On the stool next to me was a woman's purse. This is so embarrassing to admit, but I must be truthful in telling my story. I grabbed the purse and ran out the door, hoping it had a few dollars in it so that I could eat that day.

Seven guys chased me and tackled me on the hard concrete surface. I hit the ground with a thud, and they held me until the police arrived. I was arrested and brought to the police station, where I was fingerprinted and had my mug shot taken. After a few hours, they took me to Los Angeles County Jail. There they lined us all up, about thirty other men, and made us strip naked and go in a long line of showers that were ice-cold.

They gave us clothes, and we had to go to the processing station, which takes about a day and a half of waiting in lines and answering medical questions and being X-rayed. I watched guys fighting brutally, and they even had some weird ritual where two men would interlock their legs and trade punches to the face. I saw an Asian man get hit so hard that his face got broken; there was so much blood.

After a few days of this, I was taken to a cell with a cellmate. They gave me a psychological evaluation and put me on medications that did not work. The food was bad, but at least I had food, and I prayed to God to thank him before each meal. I still would rather be homeless than spend a day in jail.

Eventually I got in contact with my mom, and she put money into my account so that I could get to the commissary and buy snacks and a small pencil and paper to draw or write on. Jail life was horrible and dangerous, and being locked up was the worst thing. When I was alone in my cell, I recited a mantra I learned at a Jain hermitage and prayed every day.

Eventually they took me to see a psychiatrist. I was still very manic and paranoid, and I started screaming in his face because he would not shake my hand; I felt that this was the ultimate disrespect. In revenge, he had me transferred to cellblock 7. There I learned about a new kind of hell. It was where they put people who were suicide risks, but I was not suicidal at all, and he knew that.

This place was unbelievably draconian, like something out of a horror movie. They made me strip naked and get in a metal cell with no mattress, no bedding, no pillow, no toothbrush, and no soap or toilet paper. Just a steel cell and nothing to stop the coldness of the metal bedframe again my naked body.

Showers were only allowed about once a week. I was locked in the shower that was always ice-cold for hours, and I ended up sleeping on the floor with water running over me. Cellblock 7 was a chamber of horrors; you could hear people screaming all night. I stayed up pacing and reciting my mantra, sometimes for eight hours straight. There was no commissary in 7, so I was so hungry all the time. They eventually gave me a little bit of toilet paper to use on the steel toilet in the small cell.

They sent a beautiful young psychologist to talk to me through the bars. I was naked and embarrassed, but she was very nice to me. She told me I was going to speak to the judge at the courthouse near LAX. This experience would shock anyone. They still wouldn't give me my clothes. Instead, I had to wear a weird green suicide suit, and they wrapped me in chains.

They took me to the holding area to get the bus to court at 4:30 a.m., and I was locked into a little cage on the bus. There I saw things that were right out of a movie. Two guys, a white guy and a Black guy, were having a rapping fight. I could not believe this really happened, but it was amazing to witness. They were rapping insults to each other, and it was so cool.

In court I saw a lawyer who was appointed to me, and I saw the judge. After about three months in Los Angeles County Jail, they released to me to a jail mental hospital in another part of town.

The jail mental hospital was a world away from cellblock 7. You could smoke there about eight times a day, and they even gave you state cigarettes! It was coed, and I was locked in there with some beautiful girls. Unlike the psychiatric hospitals in New York, you were allowed to have sex there, and they even gave out free condoms.

Every room had a few beds, and each had a curtain that you could wrap around the bed for privacy. The food was really great, and you could have as much as you wanted. My therapist was smart and pretty, and it was such a relief to be away from a male-dominated environment. To me, the worst part of jail was that there were so few women to talk to. My soul is more feminine than masculine, and I have always leaned toward feminine things such as softer music and art and poetry and love and cats and nature.

Being with women again was such a wonderful thing. There was a pretty girl at the jail hospital. She was in her late twenties and she liked me. We wanted to hook up. The problem was there were these two guys who were mean and crazy and jealous of us, and they physically tried to keep us apart. They would stand guard around her and make it impossible for us to get together.

The two of them defaced the artwork that I had hung in my bedroom; they were all sketches of beautiful women. They drew in ink mustaches and other stupid things on my sketches and completely ruined them. I was really upset, but the staff refused to help me. I knew I must take matters into my own hands. During dinner, I got up from the table and ran down the hall to the living room where one of the guys was sitting with a group watching a movie. I charged at him and hit him in the head with lefts and rights. He put down in his head so that I couldn't hit him in the face and raised his knee into my crotch. I thought that with these defensive moves, he might have some martial arts training, but I overpowered him and put him in a headlock, choking him as hard as I could.

The girls who worked there started yelling at me to let him go. I finally relented and tossed him aside like the piece of trash he was. The male staff were overjoyed that I had finally done something about it. This was jail and you were on your own. I still wasn't able to hook up with the young woman, but at least I had defended myself from their bullshit.

If we'd been allowed to be together, we could have had a beautiful relationship. It would have made being locked up so much better. Love can make these places wonderful if it could have grown to that. We could have cuddled and watched movies together in the living room and spent the nights holding each other and making love. It would have been so beautiful. I still find it sad to this day, and it caused so many more problems.

As the calendar turned to the Christmas holiday season, we learned that the state had passed a law that smoking would no longer be allowed after January 1. This was so upsetting to me. Smoking is such a relief to mental patients, as we have so much underlying stress. In addition, the medicine they put me on was not working, and I was still in a manic state of mind. My mother was scheduled to visit me after the new year, and she said they might release me to her, if the judge agreed.

I was so upset having had to deal with the two jerks and now the lack of cigarettes that I decide to escape. It was probably not the best decision, but manic people are not known for making logical choices.

That night a friend of mine helped me remove a window from my bathroom one brick at a time with some tools we had stolen. We finally got the window out of the wall, and I climbed into the courtyard. I had to scale the twenty-foot chain-link fence with the barbed wire on top. I start climbing, but the guards caught me right away and brought me back to the jail mental hospital.

They yelled at me, but there wasn't much they could do, so the next night I tried again, this time wearing long socks over my hands and arms to protect me from the barbed wire. I was able to climb up the fence, over the barbed wire, and onto an adjacent rooftop. From there I jumped the twenty feet and was free. I had forty dollars in my pocket, and I made my way by bus back to Venice Beach.

There was a club there near the boardwalk where people danced and hung out. I talked to the pretty waitress, who was sweet and gave me free pizza and soda. I danced the night away and had a great time talking to people. There were cameras with big lights, so I think they might have been filming something for TV, but who knows? The next day I was alone and homeless again on the beach, but it was much better than being locked up. I could now bum cigarettes from people, but I knew I could never steal again.

I started going through the many garbage cans that lined the beach, looking for food. There were so many people there that by evening the garbage cans were literally full of food. Even though a lot of it was half eaten, it did not bother me. I just was happy to be fed. I prayed to God before each meal in thanks for the food.

The next day I walked to Santa Monica and snuck into a beach club. It was a very exclusive place, and I was able to shower, shave, and wash my hair using all their high-end products. On my way out, I saw a bunch of buffet tables that had been set up for lunch. I started eating from a leftover plate where nobody was sitting. A pool boy or whatever he was grabbed the plate from me. I told him I was homeless and had no food, but he did not care at all. This cruelty still sits badly with me when I think about it. It was just garbage, but the young man was so mean, he would not even see me as a human being.

Hanging out on the beach underneath the boardwalk late that night, I met two guys, and we started talking. They showed me a way into a passage underneath the boardwalk by moving several pieces of wood. There we shared a bottle of vodka that they had, and we smoked something out of a pipe, but I have no clue what it was. It was either crack or meth or crank or something I have never heard of, but I was tweaking big-time and eventually started walking back to Venice.

The next day on Venice Beach, a very kind man who was playing a horn gave me eighty dollars out of the goodness of his heart. It was so nice to know that there were indeed still good people out there. I bought food and a pack of cigarettes. During the day I met a beautiful Indian woman, and we had a date. We walked around together and watched the street musicians and interesting people. At the end of the date, I kissed her good night, but I had no phone and no home and no way of finding her again. It was a very good day, though.

On Thursday nights there were drum circles on Venice Beach, and I hung out there for hours, singing and drumming with a borrowed drum and talking to people. When I am manic, I am much more social, full of a false confidence that I don't have when I am stable and I'm my usually introverted self.

A few days later, I found a guy on a bench singing and playing a guitar. I sat down next to him to enjoy the music. He invited me to smoke a joint with him, and I accepted. Within minutes a bunch of cop cars pulled up and asked me for ID. I told them I had none, but they seemed to know who I was anyway and made me give them my full name or they would run my fingerprints. They entered my name in the computer, and of course I had a warrant for escaping jail. They searched me, cuffed me, and threw me in the back of the police car.

I was taken back to Los Angelos County Jail, where I went through the same fucked-up two-day initiation process with the showers with everybody watching and the medical exams and all the same bullshit. They put me back in cellblock 7, and I was again naked and alone in a steel cell with nothing else.

One night in 7, I was awakened by a dark figure entering my cell with a knife. I quickly put up my arms to defend myself. He stabbed me and then ran off. I guess I will never know who this person was or who sent him, but that cell door did not open itself, and if you don't believe this happened, I have the scar on my arm to prove it.

After a while I was taken to court again. My lawyer yelled at me for escaping, and the judge was not pleased either. I spent about three more months in jail until I was released to a rooming house in Venice for the mentally disabled. There I was expected to attend a program during the day. I thought it was going to be okay but then I met the woman in charge of the house, and she was completely out of her mind. She was a like a Nazi, nasty and cruel. She wouldn't let me smoke when I wanted or even move from the chair she put me in. She told me to lie in bed and watch TV, but she would not even let me pick the channel.

The people who brought me to the house gave me their number because I guess they realized I was being set up by someone who did not like me much, and they figured I might be able to request a different house. I'd had enough of this Nazi bitch after a few hours but could not find the number for the people who'd brought me there, so I just grabbed my meds and headed back to the beach.

I continued to eat out of garbage cans and sleep on the beach, and I was happy to not be in jail anymore. One night I watched a Pink Floyd cover band at Danny's, and I sat with an older couple who give me food and soda. I had a very good night.

I went to the Venice library a lot, where I would sit at the computer with my headphones and check email and listen to and watch music videos. My favorite videos were Avril Lavigne's love songs off her *Goodbye Lullaby* album. This brought me a lot of peace.

One day at the library, I was talking to a homeless young woman when this big muscled Black guy started yelling at me that she was his girlfriend and that I better get the hell out of there. He also told me that he was a security guard, which I didn't believe. I thought he was just a crazy person.

I slept on the side of the library some nights, and one day I had a manic delusion that some blankets I found were a gift for me. The blankets were brown and black with lions all over them and seemed really expensive. Of course, with my luck they turned out to be owned by the so-called security guard, who started screaming at me, then he slapped me really hard in the face. I was stunned and scared, and I did not know what to do. He told me I better leave Venice Beach.

The next day I was on the boardwalk, and the big scary Black dude was there with five of his friends. They told me I better leave the beach immediately. I felt that they would jump me in private if I walked to Santa Monica and that I would be safer around the people in Venice.

One guy chased me on a bicycle and hit me in the legs with a huge stick. I fell down and was scared but unhurt. Then three other guys approached me. One threw a punch at my face, but I punched back. Our fists hit each other, and they broke off their attack.

Then a different dude ran at me throwing punches, which I returned, and we started rolling around on the ground fighting. At first, he was on top of me, but I got the upper hand and turned him around to start winning the fight. I was on top of him throwing punches when the so-called security guard grabbed me tightly by the ear and dragged me away to the alley. He pushed me against the building and started throwing rights at my face. He hit me over and over again really hard, and I was frozen with fear. I'd never been more afraid.

He hit me at least nine times but then stopped when he became exhausted from punching me. I didn't know what to do, so I got down on my knees and put my hands together and prayed to God for help. With renewed strength, I ran at him. I wrapped my legs around his body so that he couldn't punch me anymore, and I started to choke him with both hands. This went on for a few moments and then I passed out. When I woke, he and his friends were gone.

I finally left Venice Beach and walked back to Santa Monica. I was a bloody mess from the fighting, and I was exhausted. I talked to some firemen on the beach and told them that the judge could go fuck himself. I got them to call an ambulance. In the emergency room, they fed me and said I was suffering from exposure on top of being beaten up. I started shaking—my whole body was releasing all the stored-up fear and energy of the last few days. They gave me some orange juice, and I was momentarily happy.

Just as I was getting some rest, a bunch of cops burst in and pulled me from the gurney, cuffed me, and took me back to LA County Jail on a warrant for leaving the rooming house. There was a riot going on in the jail and everything was crazy. I sat in a room with a bunch of guys for hours and hours, waiting for the corrections officers to quell the riot. Eventually they threw me back in cellblock 7, where I was once again stripped down and left naked in the cell without bedding or anything but the hard cold steel of the room.

I went to court after a few days, and my lawyer yelled at me for leaving the program and the judge yelled at me and told me to go back to New York City, even if I had to go through Canada. This was virtually impossible because I had no ID. Without ID in this country, you are a nonentity, and travel by plane or bus or train is impossible.

Soon, I was transferred to a so-called normal jail cell, and I was able to draw and write at night with things I bought from the commissary with the money my mother had put in for me. I paced a lot in my little cell, and even though they let us go out during the day to the wider cellblock, I mostly kept to myself and didn't socialize too much. I spent many hours saying the Namokar mantra, which I learned from the Jain monk in New Jersey. I was kept in jail a few more months and then they surprised me one early morning by letting me out. Apparently overcrowding was a big issue in this state, and they just let me out onto the street.

I knew I needed to get out of California and go home to New York City, so I immediately found a pay phone and called my mom. She sent me some money by Western Union and bought me an Amtrak train ticket back to New York, but because I had no ID, I couldn't board the train. An extremely kindhearted police officer decided to help me and talked to the train officials. He vouched for me, and they let me board. Finally, after two years of crazy times, I left California.

Chapter 3

ALBUQUERQUE, NEW MEXICO

(2011)

I got on the train to New York City with a transfer in Chicago, and I hated it. In my manic state, I found it impossible to sit in my seat, so I spent most of my time in the lounge car watching the beautiful scenery and sleeping on the floor. I smoked cigarettes in the bathroom when I could and bought some chips and soda in the bar area downstairs from the lounge car with the few dollars I had.

When the train stopped in Albuquerque, a train official approached and asked for ID. I explained that I didn't have any, and he told me the conductor wanted me off the train. Two cops boarded and said I had to leave if I couldn't present an ID. I reluctantly got off in the desert town. The female cop was very sweet and gave me five dollars to get a sandwich.

ALBUQUERQUE, NEW MEXICO

Now I was stranded in a town I had never been to and knew nothing about. I called my mom, and after a lot of hard work, she got me into a small motel room, convincing the owners to let her pay by credit card over the phone. She had to fax them her ID and credit card and other paperwork so that I had a place to stay for a week. During this time, we attempted to get my birth certificate from New York so that I could try to get an ID from the Albuquerque DMV.

I went into a local phone store and got a free phone. I now had some way to communicate with the outside world. I began exploring the city and looking at the various stores and restaurants. I was enjoying motel life and found many nice people to talk to. There were a lot of truckers at the motel, along with a few families and other people. I called my cousin the doctor, and she phoned in my psych meds to a local pharmacy. I was taking them but was still experiencing mania.

After a week at the motel, we still couldn't get an ID. My mom said she was not paying for any more motel rooms and to go to the mental hospital or to a homeless shelter. So, I was quickly homeless again. My uncle sent me $300, and I purchased a guitar from a local music shop for $150. With the rest I bought food and cigarettes.

I liked to go to Starbucks and either draw or write poetry and drink coffee. I used their bathrooms to wash up in every day to try to stay clean. I began hanging out at the University of Albuquerque campus, and I found a beautiful piano to play in the large lounge and eating area. I played a lot of what I could remember, and a gay dude gave me a music book full of amazing songs. I was so grateful and happy for the gift.

One day I went to a church picnic they were throwing for the homeless. I ate well and talked to nice people. They gave me a blanket, which made me so happy because it gets very cold at night in the desert. I slept a lot on campus near a lake. One night a drunk homeless guy approached me there. He was very cold, so I shared the blanket with him, and we huddled up on a bench for the night.

Another time I was walking alone on the main street at about three or four o'clock in the morning when a car slowly passed by me. Inside it were three Black youths. The one in the back took out a gun and shot at me, then they sped off. Because you are reading this book, I guess you can surmise he missed. It just makes me wonder how people can be so cruel, trying to kill someone they don't even know and valuing life and its preciousness so little.

I hung out more on campus because it felt safer to me and because there were so many cool people around. One day I met a pretty student in the lounge, and we got to talking. We made a date to hang out at the library that evening. We sat and talked for hours, and it was just so wonderful to be with a beautiful and intelligent woman and to forget my deep troubles for a while. At the end we hugged goodbye, but of course I never saw her again.

I was directed to find a social services place that provided food, clothes, and safety during the day, and I hung out there for a while. I went to the library nearby, and an amazing girl who worked there gave me a library card using the address from the social services place. I now had some ID! I can't explain to you how much a small kindness like that meant to me in my hours of despair and loneliness.

The ID changed everything for me because now I could go to the homeless shelter and they would let me in. The shelter was kind of awful, though, and very dangerous, and the food was disgusting, so I did not stay there for more than a night or two. Soon, with my ID and a very helpful person at the bus station, my sister paid for my ticket, and I was on my way to my parents' condo in Boca Raton, Florida.

In the bus station, I met a beautiful woman of about twenty-eight. She was traveling to Houston to pick up her car. We struck up a friendship, and she wanted me to smoke pot with her outside. I didn't really want to, but she blew it in my face, thinking it was funny. We sat together on the bus, and she gave me rules about physical affection because she'd had some bad experiences. We cuddled and slept well during the night.

This kind, sweet, beautiful woman helped me so much to get to my parents' place. I was tired, confused, and not mentally well, and she helped me transfer to all the right buses until she got off in Houston. I had to take four buses to get to Florida. Once there, my mom picked me up and took me home to her condo.

Chapter 4

CHILDHOOD

Let's backtrack a bit to see where all of this started. One of my fondest childhood memories is from about nine years of age. I was sitting on the floor of my bedroom in my house on Staten Island pondering the universe. I was trying to picture the entire universe in my head, but it was unfathomable. I wanted to know, if this universe is everything, what's on the other side? How can it be endless, and what was it contained in? I clearly remember tears running down my cheeks as I contemplated the sheer enormity of everything. I could not understand how something could be so immense yet not be infinite. Who created this and why? The thought of it awed me.

I was an extremely active and wild child. I got into everything, and my family needed to watch me constantly so that I would not hurt myself or break something. My mother had me tested, and she was told that I was hyperactive and that they could put me on medication. My parents decided against this. The doctor also said I was superintelligent but very immature.

I loved sports most of all. I was in Little League from a very early age. My coach thought I should have my eyes tested. He said I was very athletic, but for some reason I could not hit the ball the right way. In the second grade, I was fitted for glasses, and this solved many problems. I started to excel at athletics, and I was very into baseball, football and tennis and paddleball.

Sundays were for football. It was like a religion to me. Every Sunday I would go down to the den and prepare for a day of football. I would start with the 12:30 p.m. pregame show and continue all day with two games and then the after-game show. I not only watched the games but also kept a notebook in which to record the statistics for every game of the season. I would count every pass, attempted and completed, as well as rushing yards and penalties and every single stat I could think of. In my own way, I was doing analytics before it ever became a thing. At the end of the season, I would compile the stats and come out with all kinds of relevant numbers.

Even though I was a New Yorker, my favorite team as a child was the Dallas Cowboys. I loved the Jets too, but it was the 1970s, and my number one team was the Cowboys. I think it was the uniforms I liked the most, especially the helmets. I thought the star on the helmets was supercool. Roger Staubuck was my favorite player and quarterback, and I thought Tom Landry was a great coach in his suit and hat. As I got older, the Jets became my team, and I forgot all about the Cowboys.

At age eleven I was with my cousin, who lived across the street, and we were walking his dog at about nine o'clock at night when a bunch of drunken teenagers started throwing rocks at us. A large stone hit me in the head, and I screamed and fell to the ground in what felt like slow motion. There was blood everywhere, and my cousin said I looked like Frankenstein.

My father heard me screaming and came running out of the house. He picked me up and carried me back home. The teenagers dispersed. In the house I calmed down and asked my father if I could look in the mirror. What I saw was not pretty: There was a huge hole in my forehead, and I could literally see my skull. My parents took me to the emergency room, and I wanted my father to come into the room with me for the stitches. I held his hand tightly as they put shot after shot into the wound. I could not believe how many needles were required to clean and numb the area. But I didn't cry; I just closed my eyes and squeezed my father's hand.

X-rays showed I did not have a broken skull, but I did need thirty stitches to close up the injury, and I had a concussion. At home the next day, a police officer came to take a report, but the teenagers were never found. This incident had a profound effect on my life and not in a good way. I became anxious and was afraid to leave the house for years. I would go to school, but otherwise I would not leave the house without prodding from my parents. Eventually I was able to play on the street around me, but the anxiety was really severe for many years.

By puberty I developed social anxiety and severe body dysmorphia. I thought I was the ugliest thing in the world and that no girl would ever love me. It did not help that I had a small mole under my nose that seemed to me to be as big as a football. I hated it so much; I was so embarrassed. I had acne as well, which just made things worse.

I remember in intermediate school, I would take off my glasses so that I would not be able to see the expression of disgust on the girls' faces when they looked at me in the hallways. I was sure I was a hideous monster. It was so upsetting to me because all I really wanted out of life was love. I fell in love with different girls all the time, and I just wanted to hold them and to be held and to have a loving relationship and romance. I thought it would never happen with my hideous face.

In sixth grade this cute girl wanted to be my girlfriend, and I really liked her. She said to me, "I want to go out with you." I was still convinced I was ugly, and I thought she was making fun of me. No matter how hard she tried, I could not be convinced. I really did like her. She was a cute, smart, and funny girl. If I just would have believed her, she could have saved me.

When I was about five years old, my parents bought a piano for the house. My sisters took lessons, but the teacher said he could not teach me because I was too wild. He did not even try, and as a piano teacher myself, I am horrified by this. I have never in all my years of teaching piano or guitar denied a child at least a chance to learn. I have taught autistic children and children with severe ADHD and other disabilities, and I would never do what he did. I resented it then and I still do now.

I decided at this tender age that I would teach myself despite the judgment of this so-called piano teacher. I started looking through my sisters' music books, and I asked them what the notes meant. One sister told me to remember "Every Good Boy Does Fine and FACE." These letters correspond to the treble clef. I figured the left hand out on my own and started to read chords based on the letter of the chord. I don't really remember exactly how I did it, but I was determined to play. Over the years I got better and better and learned how to accompany myself singing, which become a love of mine.

I was very influenced by the piano players of the day, especially Barry Manilow, Billy Joel, and Elton John. I would sometimes watch Liberace on *The Tonight Show Starring Johnny Carson*, and he was a huge inspiration to me. I loved the way he played. Playing piano and singing became an escape for me. For hours I would play mostly love songs and dream about the girls I was in love with. I did not get any encouragement at home for my playing, but when I took some lessons for about four months during my senior year in high school, my teacher told me that if I'd started with him at eight, I would have been a concert pianist. This still haunts me.

I was very wild at school and constantly got into trouble. In sixth grade I lit off a pack of firecrackers in a locker and had to go to the dean for a day of interrogation and detention. On another occasion when we had a substitute teacher, I threw a desk out the window of the third-floor classroom. I had lots of friends, both male and female, but I was extremely lonely. I wanted a girlfriend and a loving romantic relationship more than anything in the world. I prayed to God to give me a beautiful girlfriend.

I had a big crush on this girl in my class, Scarlett. She had long beautiful hair and blue eyes, and I wanted so badly to be with her. On one occasion one of my best friends, Olivia, who was friends with Scarlett and a male friend of mine, all went to the mall together. I did not say a word to Scarlett because I was nervous and shy. Olivia kept saying to both of us, "Just talk to each other!" But the words would not come out of my mouth. I was horrified and embarrassed that I could not get up the courage to form a sentence and talk to this girl.

I would spend hours on the phone talking to my friend Emma, sometimes until my ear turned red. I had so much to say, but if I liked somebody romantically, I was completely silenced by anxiety. Emma always had boyfriends, and she would tell me about her sex life.

I played trumpet in the school band but was not very good at it, earning myself a third trumpet designation. I did not hate the trumpet, but I guess I was not that great at practicing. The teacher was very sarcastic and not that cool. I continued to play piano at home; that was the instrument I loved.

I secretly wrote a lot of poetry and never showed anybody. Later in life, when I was in my thirties, I became a published poet and got paid for it, which I thought was pretty amazing. I wrote a story in class one day about my little sister having cancer and that we used to make cupcakes together and share so much but then she died in the hospital. The teacher broke down crying and called my mother in sympathy, but my mom had to explain that I did not have a little sister and that I had made the whole thing up. I thought it was quite hilarious, but at least it showed good writing skills.

I played sports all the time; it was my biggest passion. I played Little League in the spring and tackle football with my friends in the fall and winter. During the summers it was more baseball with my friends and tennis or paddleball at the swim club we belonged to.

The school field day came in the fifth grade, and I was sure I was the fastest in my school. There was another boy, John S., who thought he was faster than me, and we argued about it all the time until the day of the race came. I was confident that I would be victorious and shut up John S. for good. We were at the starting line—John, myself, and about seven other kids—when a terrible thing happened. They used a starter pistol, which I was not prepared for at all, and I totally missed the start.

Even though I was behind all the other kids, I ran for my life and caught up and passed everybody but John, who finished just in front of me. I was so pissed! No matter how much I complained, John was now the fastest at school, and I could do nothing about it. John had bragging rights for real now, and boy, he never let me forget it.

For picture day in the fifth grade, everyone was dressed smartly in their finest clothes. My good friend Chloe, who sat next me, was wearing a beautiful black velvet dress. For some reason that escapes me now, I decided that it would be a great idea to glue her to her seat, so I put a ton of Elmers glue on her chair before she sat down. When she could not get up without tearing her dress, I laughed so hard I thought my sides would split. The teacher, Chloe, and her mom did not think it was so funny, and I heard about it for years afterward.

During these early years, I had a great love for science, especially astronomy. I read all of Carl Sagan's books and anything on astronomy and physics. I watched the miniseries *Cosmos* on PBS and loved anything science related. I even had a subscription to *Science Digest*.

I loved to learn and read every day for hours and hours. Even at bedtime, I would sneak a flashlight under the covers and read until the break of dawn. In school, during math class or others I was not interested in, I would keep my science book on my lap and read while the teacher spoke.

I did just enough schoolwork to pass, and I copied the homework from friends. I hated school with a passion, even though I loved to learn. For one thing, it was too early in the morning, and I was and still am a night owl. They also taught things I was not interested in, like math or Spanish. I hated sitting there when I could be home playing sports or reading the books I wanted to read.

When I was twelve, I read *The Origin of Species* by Charles Darwin, and I loved it. I got into quantum physics and Einstein, and if I did not have the money, I would simply steal the books from the bookstore. Reading was my first love, even more than sports and music. If I really loved a book, it was not unusual for me to read all day, sometimes up to twelve hours straight. I still love books today, even if I can't quite read that many hours anymore. Books are more valuable than gold to me, and when I had my last nervous breakdown and got rid of over a thousand of my books, it still breaks my heart to this day when I think about it. I feel it's something mental illness took from me, and I can never replace those books.

In the fourth grade, my best friend and I decided to walk into an opening into the sewer system and go exploring. We took a flashlight and wore our boots and walked through a maze of sewer pipes that went on for miles. Eventually we were very lost and had to climb up a ladder to a manhole cover and push it open. When we emerged, we had no idea where we were, so we found a phone booth to call my mom, and she picked us up.

It was not until a few days later when this trip into stupidity really reared its ugly head. I became very ill and could not hold down any food and had a fever. The doctor discovered I had rickettsia, a form of Rocky Mountain spotted fever. The only way to get it those days was to be bitten by a flea that had been on a rat. I was sick for months and missed a lot of school, which I did not care about anyway. I had a teacher that year I greatly disliked. I wanted to be in the class with the pretty, sweet, kind blonde-haired teacher who we all loved. Instead, I was put in the class with the evil teacher.

Eventually I recovered but then got mononucleosis later that year. Fourth grade was just a wash of illness. I hated doing the blood tests every week for the duration of the illness. One day at the doctor's office, I decided to lock myself in the bathroom instead of going for my weekly blood test. It took at least an hour of the nurses and doctors banging at the door for me to come out and face the needle. I was only eleven and needles were scary, especially every week for months.

The worst part of having mono, though, was that my spleen was enlarged, and I could not play tackle football because they said if I got hit in that area, my spleen could burst, and I would die. Even though I knew better, I played tackle football anyway, but my mom caught me and freaked out. From then on, I become the coach, and I even had my own clipboard. Otherwise, I think my parents would have tied me to the bed.

In elementary school my good friend Jim and I decided to try to get on the roof. I was able to turn the lock open using a pencil, and up we went. We discovered a litany of objects that we decided to throw at the children and people four stories below. We found mostly tennis balls and other balls and had a great time chucking them down onto the heads of unsuspecting people.

In another adventure Jim and I went into the school basement to explore a bit of the janitors' quarters. I think we were looking for *Playboy* magazines, but we found something nearly as cool—an acetylene torch. We decided to steal it and make our own fires. Jim and I loved fire! Every year we saved our allowances to buy hundreds of dollars' worth of fireworks in the summer. We would shoot them off at the oncoming cars on the expressway or at houses, but our main prize was to shoot rockets at passing helicopters.

With the torch, our love of fire moved to a whole new level, and we started burning our names into fences and all kinds of things. We set fire after fire. I don't remember what happened to the torch. I think Jim took it home and that was the last I saw of it.

Jim and I were hanging out by the school one day when I heard a soft meow. It was a beautiful black-and-white kitten. We played with her and petted her for a long time but then it got dark and we had to go. We started to walk back to my house, but this little kitten was determined and followed us home. I would stop to pet her, but she kept following us no matter what we did. I picked her up and brought her home.

My mom said we absolutely could not keep her because we had a dog and because she was allergic to cats. I asked if we could keep the kitty in the garage until we found her a home. My mom said yes but only until she was adopted. So, Kitty spent her nights in the garage, and we fed her some kitten food we bought. I guess you can tell by where this is heading that Kitty moved in lock, stock, and barrel and became our beloved family cat for the next sixteen wonderful years. That day changed my life forever.

Chapter 5

CAMP CEJWIN

(1983-1984)

During my childhood I spent two summers at a Jewish camp in upstate New York. The first year I went for only four weeks. I was about twelve or thirteen then, and I was excited to go away with my two best friends at the time, Benjamin and Ethan. We all shared a love of sports, especially baseball, and we looked forward to playing as much as possible.

The camp was kosher, and I did not love the food at all. One day I decided to sneak the two miles or so to the main gate and order a real pizza from the pay phone there. Using the phone book in the booth, I found a local pizzeria in a nearby town. I ordered the pizza and waited at the gate for it to be delivered, then paid the man with money I had.

I was so psyched to finally have real food, and pizza has always been my favorite. When it was delivered, I knew if any staff member found me with the nonkosher food, they would confiscate it. I ran full speed all the way back to my bunk and returned safely without my precious meal being stolen. I was sweating, as it was a hot summer day, and the bunks had no air-conditioning.

A few of my fellow bunkmates were there, but most of them were out playing sports. I proceeded to eat all eight slices in rapid succession before my counselor or anyone else could take it from me. It was only a few minutes after swallowing the whole pie that I started to feel sick and queasy. After all that anticipation and waiting and running and trouble to get some real pizza, I threw it all up. I was meticulous in my aim and made sure I threw up on the freshly made bed of a kid who I was not particularly fond of. He was not happy when he returned to the bunk, and his mother made mean faces at me during visitors' day. I still don't why I was so cruel sometimes.

When I was packing to go to the camp, I decided to bring my grandfather's bayonet from World War I. It was hidden deep in my parents' closet, but I always liked to explore, and I was fascinated by the weapon. One day I was showing my bunkmates the bayonet, but somebody reported it to the staff, and it was confiscated immediately. My parents were not happy with that phone call.

The first half of that summer was uneventful, but I made friends with a dark-haired girl who had written Duran, Duran on her legs in sunscreen and then laid out in the sun. Now her legs had the band's name on them for the summer. We became very good friends and kept in touch all year by letter and telephone.

I loved to play tennis and was in the camp tournament. I did very well but lost in the finals to a superior player. It was fun, although I got very nervous before each match. Ben and Ethan were not that into tennis, but we had a great time every day playing other sports like softball and basketball.

The staff let me play the piano in the dining area when it was empty, so I had some fun and had brought music with me. I would read and listen to music in my spare time and enjoyed the rafting activities on the lake. We would take out the big orange rafts and play war games by splashing one another and trying to sink one another's rafts. It was a lot of fun. I liked swimming too, and the lake was a great place to hang out.

I had a good time that first summer, so Ben, Ethan, and I decided to come back the next year for the full seven weeks. The next summer was not as much fun as the first because there were now nighttime activities with the girls. I had social phobia and was usually very shy around girls. I made excuses every time not to go to these evening events. It just made me too nervous. I would stay in the bunk and read, including the sci-fi classic *Battlefield Earth* by L. Ron Hubbard.

Ben had found a girlfriend, and he would sneak out in the middle of the night to her bunk so that they could fool around. I think the staff kind of looked the other way at these things.

On an overnight excursion to the island in the middle of the lake, I got up the courage to talk to the two prettiest girls in camp. Soon, Ethan joined me, and we put our sleeping bags and packs near them. I asked the girls if they would like to go for a walk with us, and they agreed. The walk was fun, and we talked and laughed freely.

They stepped away from us for a few minutes to pee, and I told Ethan that I thought they liked us and that we should try to kiss them that night. Ethan said he liked one over the other, but he was nervous too and could not make up his mind. I thought they were both beautiful, but I let him psych me out and we did not try.

We did talk to them a lot, though, and slept near them, but we both regretted for years our missed opportunity. In the camp yearbook at the end of the summer, the girl who Ethan liked listed his initials for who she was in love with.

Most of our time was spent playing sports. In one memorable softball game against a visiting camp, I was playing second base and Ethan was playing shortstop, with Ben setting up at third base. We always did well in these games, and in this particular one, I was up with men on base, and I hit a ball right down the left field line that I ran all the way around for a home run. We ended up winning the game. We were so happy and celebrated the rest of the day.

My friend from the summer before who I stayed in contact with all year had made sure to get her cousin Lucas in our bunk because she thought we would be nice to him. Unfortunately, it did not work out that way. Lucas had a cleft palate and was a very obnoxious child. We did not make fun of his disability, but we were not very nice to him either. If fact, we could be quite mean to him. He was not bullied or harmed physically, but he was picked on. He was such an annoying personality. I stopped talking to my friend all summer because I was mad that she had her cousin put in our bunk.

Every morning, we all got up early and lined up for announcements and such. They would give us the scores of the Yankees and Mets games from the night before, as we did not have televisions in our bunks.

Our bunk counselor, Lenny, was only eighteen, but at that time he seemed so grown up. He showed me pictures of his girlfriend, who was very beautiful and went to Vassar College. I really looked up to him and thought he was such a cool guy. He got me into some new music I had never heard, including the Violent Femmes and Run-DMC.

In one incident with Lucas, we got into an argument, and I was mouthing off to him pretty good. The camp director was called in, and he told me I have a cruel mouth. He said he was going to take me to the office to write me up, and I replied, "Fine with me, motherfucker!"

One day while Lucas and I were alone and talking, we decided to check out the bunk next to us. I liked to explore and was curious about the older kids' bunk. Why I brought Lucas with me I will never know, but we went in their bunk and were looking around, and I found a locked box next to one kid's bed. I hunted for the key and found it very quickly.

I opened the box, and inside were two twenty-dollar bills. I was thinking I could get this toy I wanted when I got home and proceeded to steal the money. I don't know what was wrong with me. I was fourteen years old, and I probably could have gotten the toy from my parents if I had asked for it enough. It's one of the mysteries of my childhood because I made such stupid decisions sometimes. Stealing the money was bad enough, but doing it with Lucas as a witness was just as stupid because he hated me.

The theft was a very big deal at the camp, and a general assembly was called by the camp director to address the matter. Eventually they decided to allow the money to be returned with no questions asked that day. But Lucas ratted me out before I could return it, and I was called before the camp director.

He basically threatened me physically and dared me to hit him over it. I was fourteen, and he was a full-grown man in his thirties, and I was shocked by the incident. But the worst was yet to come.

Later that day, Stan, the kid whose money I had stolen, along with his whole bunk, came into my bunk to extract their revenge. In a scene right out of *Lord of the Flies*, all ten of them surrounded me and started pushing me. Ben was there and tried to pull them off me and make the fight between just Stan and me. I was in my underwear, and I was overcome with fear for my life. Ben ended up being six foot five and 220 pounds as an adult, so he was by far the biggest and strongest of all the children. Eventually all the other kids in the bunk surrounded Stan and me as we squared off to fight. It became mostly a wrestling match, as Stan was older than me and at least a half a head taller. We locked hands and proceeded to fight as the other boys screamed around us, cheering Stan on. I was scared to death, but I fought him the best I could. I was surprised by how strong I was and that he could not overpower me completely. He did get me to the ground, though, and my knees were bleeding badly.

In time the fight broke up, and they went back to their bunk with a warning to me about no reprisals against Lucas. I was physically hurt in the fight, but mostly it was my pride that was severely damaged. I was so ashamed and scared. I thought of myself as a coward and that I should have kicked his ass. At that tender age, I did not understand a lot of things.

I was a nervous child generally, but I thought I was just being a coward. I confused fear with lack of courage. It was not until I was much older that I finally realized that everyone has fear and that to act within that fear is what courage is. This incident had a huge effect on my self-esteem. I hated myself and was ashamed for years over it. I never told my parents.

On the last day of camp, my parents came to pick me up. My female friend from the previous summer finally came to talk to me. It was the first time we'd spoken all summer. She told me she'd had a huge crush on me the whole two years and wanted to be my girlfriend. I was so mad at her for putting her cousin Lucas in our bunk that it killed our friendship, even though I did not feel the same romantic feelings toward her. She was a great person and a true friend, so I just told her that I liked her too. We never spoke again.

Chapter 6

HIGH SCHOOL

(1984-1988)

I went to Susan E. Wagner High School in Staten Island. After not doing that well or paying much attention in intermediate school, I decided I wanted to make a change and give a good effort in high school. I was attentive and did my work properly, and I was rewarded at the end of the first term with a 95.33 GPA, which was good enough for ninth in the school.

Because of this they moved me into the Scholars' Academy for the second term, and all the classes were much harder. I still managed a 91.6 GPA, and I was very pleased with my work and my life. Things seemed to be going better for me. That freshman year I tried out for the baseball team with Ethan and Ben; they were chosen, but I did not make the final cut.

I was very unhappy to not be with my two best friends and to have to spend the afternoons alone in the spring. I tried out for the tennis team as well, and even though I won all my matches, I did not make that team either. I had heard the coach did not like to pick freshmen, but I was pissed off.

I had a lot of friends there from intermediate school, but I was still shy around pretty girls and did not have a girlfriend. I decided not to play baseball in Little League that year for the first time since I was seven. I did have a lonelier life without my two best friends, but I hung out with some of the kids from the Scholars' Academy.

There was a senior in my Spanish class who sat in front of me. He was a big bully and tried to intimidate me by talking trash to me every day. Finally, I'd had enough of him, and I screamed at him, "Fuck you, motherfucker!" I kept yelling at him until the teacher had to stop the class.

The bully looked at me incredulously and said, "What, are you crazy? I'll kill you!"

"Good. Kill me," I said. "Just shut the fuck up already." After that he started to like me and talked to me as a friend.

I was in love with the girl who sat next to me in history class, and I was dying to get to know her. I was so shy around her, though, and I could never think of anything to say. So, every day I asked her to borrow a pen and then I gave it back at the end of class. This went on all year, and I was so frustrated and embarrassed by my lack of confidence and my inability to have a normal conversation with her. She was so beautiful.

I read a tremendous amount when I was home and continued to play and sing at my piano. I wrote poems as well. I still wanted to be an astronomer, and most of what I read was astronomy and physics. I was still wearing braces and glasses, and I had very little confidence or self-esteem regarding my looks. A beautiful girlfriend was all I wanted, but I was too shy to ask anyone out.

My second year in high school, I made the brand-new junior varsity baseball team. It's a strange thing, but I have no memory at all of that year, especially being on the baseball team. I know I played and did not get kicked off, but it's like the whole thing never happened. I do know my grades started to drop as I lost interest in school. The first term of sophomore year, I had an 81 GPA, but the second term I made only a 71 GPA. They threw me out of the Scholars' Academy, which did not really bother me, except I had made a lot of cool friends there.

I got involved with a musical production and competition between the grades called Sing. I did not try out for band because I did not think I was good enough, and I really had never played with any other musicians. I had played alone all of my life. I decided to join the stage crew because I liked building things. My good friend ran for stage crew director when I was not there and told people to vote for me too. Somehow, I became the stage crew director with him. I would never have had the courage to campaign alone.

I really hated school by this time, mostly because it was early in the morning, and I have always been a night owl. I was very against alcohol and drugs at that age, and I was a staunch atheist as well. I did believe in ESP and other psychic phenomena, though, and I read a lot about it. I believed in science as a religion at that point. A good friend and I even talked about starting an atheist newsletter.

By the second term of junior year, my marks were plummeting. Even though I had made the varsity baseball team, I was kicked off for failing three classes.

The year was 1986, and my beloved New York Mets had made the playoffs and advanced to the World Series. There were a certain number of tickets available to the public via Ticketron, and I waited until 6:00 p.m., which was when the tickets went on sale. I had a new phone with a redial button, and I laid in my bed and pressed redial over and over again but continued to get a busy signal.

This did not deter me, as I was totally dedicated to getting my two tickets. Ethan and Ben were supposed to be doing the same thing on their end. I pressed redial from 6:00 p.m. all the way until 11:43 p.m. when I struck gold and got through by some unimaginable luck. There were only tickets left for a possible game seven, so I bought those two tickets and figured I would probably never get to use them.

But the Mets were magical that year, and in playing the Boston Red Sox in the World Series, they got to game six, which is now cemented in baseball lore. They were down some runs in the bottom of the ninth with two out and two strikes, but by some miracle and a ball going through first baseman Bill Buckner's legs, the Mets came back and won the game. I was so excited and jumped so high that I hit my head on the den ceiling. There would be a game seven after all and I was going!

I chose to take Ethan with my other ticket only because he had tried for hours as well and Ben had not. Ethan was more of a Yankees fan, but he still was dying to go to the game. Game seven was amazing. We sat in the second level. The Mets were down by a few runs and then mounted a furious comeback. With men on base, Keith Hernandez hit a single to right center, and the crowd went absolutely wild. I have never heard anything so loud in my life. I was beside myself with joy. Eventually the Mets pulled ahead, and the game was saved by relief pitcher Jesse Orosco. He threw his glove in the air, and the Mets were the champions of the world for the first time in my life.

Getting home on the subway was completely nuts. Every time the train made a stop, you could hear the whole city screaming and yelling. It was definitely one of the best days of my life.

The next day Ethan and I skipped school to go to the ticker tape parade in Manhattan. It was total chaos and anarchy. I saw people being trampled and cars being overturned and people throwing objects like phone books out the windows. I almost got trampled in the crowd and had to jump on top of a Hertz truck to stay safe. So many people were on top of the truck that the roof caved in. I jumped off so that I was not impaled by the tearing metal.

Ethan and I completely lost each other, and I made my way back alone to the ferry and to Staten Island. That was the last parade I ever went to, and I will never do that again, even if the Mets manage to win another championship, which has not happened in the thirty-eight years since.

I got my driver's license during the winter term of my junior year. My sister passed down to me my grandma's old car, and I fell in love with it. It reminded me of the 1960s and was a muscle car of that era. It was a 1969 Oldsmobile Cutlass S with a 350 engine and was superfast. I started to restore it and make it faster. I took off the faded blue original paint with a chemical peal and painted it with black primer. Then I bought new racing wheels and tires with the raised white letters and had the windows tinted limousine black. The car was starting to look really cool.

At some point I named the car Butch, and it became almost a part of me. I still had not found a girlfriend, so I spent all my time working on Butch. I had my first job working at Waldbaum's grocery store, which I hated, but at least it kept me with enough money to maintain my car rebuild expenses. I started hanging out more with my friend Patrick, who also was a car guy, although he was much more advanced than I was because his father taught him everything. He had a totally restored 1965 Ford Mustang, which was absolutely beautiful in white with a blue racing stripe.

Patrick taught me a lot about cars, and he would come over some nights with his friend who had another car from the muscle car era, a Dodge Challenger, which was really cool. One night the three of us changed the manifold and carburetor on Butch from a stock two barrels to a Holly 750 CFM four barrel, which took its toll on my gas prices but made Butch much faster. We had our little car club, and it was a huge part of my life.

I have two female first cousins who are around my age, and I was very close to them in high school. I used to sleep over sometimes on the weekend, as they lived about an hour away in Jackson, New Jersey. On one of these occasions, the younger cousin's friend Tiffany was there and sleeping over as well. She was beautiful, with blonde hair and light-brown eyes, and I had a huge crush on her.

Apparently, she felt the same way, as she flirted with me quite openly all day. She drew a smiley face on my hand and pushed me into the pool with my contact lenses on, and they floated out of my eyes. Luckily, I had my glasses with me as a backup. That night we all hung out in the guest room where I would be sleeping and watched a movie. Tiffany and I were sitting on the bed, and my cousins were in front of us.

Under the blanket Tiffany took my hand and started making little circles with her fingers. Eventually we were holding hands secretly. At one point she disengaged with my hand to lift up her shirt and pop open her bra with the front clasp. She grabbed my hand again, pulled it up her shirt, and put my hand on her breasts. Now things were getting very interesting, and I was really happy. I was so in love with her, and she was so hot.

When the movie ended, the girls went to their bedrooms to sleep. I waited awhile and then went into Tiffany's room. I asked her to come hang out with me. She agreed and returned to my bedroom while my cousins slept. We sat there for a long time, and I knew she wanted me to kiss her, but I was so nervous because I had never French kissed before. Eventually she told me she was getting tired and was going back to her bed to sleep, so I finally got up the courage and made my move to kiss her.

She was lying down on the bed, and I put my lips to hers. We opened our mouths, and it was like pure heaven. I really did not know exactly how to kiss, but our tongues intertwined, and I just followed her lead. It was the most beautiful moment of my life. We made out for a long time. To finally have my first real kiss at sixteen and with someone so beautiful was magical. It was the highlight of my life then. Eventually the kiss was over, and she went back to her room. As she left, she gently touched my bare foot and smiled at me. This was a life-changing moment for me, even though I knew she had kissed many boys before me.

For the next few months, I was literally walking on air. Tiffany was all I could think of. I thought about her twenty-four hours a day and nothing else. I was a very sensitive and romantic teenager, so this was the high point of my life. I had dreamed about making out with a beautiful girl, but the actual reality was so much better than a dream.

I even was in a good mood at the supermarket where I worked, and the hours flew by as I relived in my mind every single moment of our time together over and over. I was totally and completely in love.

Although working at the supermarket really sucked, it did have some benefits. During my junior year of high school, I had given up my policy of no drugs and alcohol and started drinking heavily on the weekends with my friends. They would come in and buy case after case of Budweiser, and I would give it to them extra cheap, as I knew we all would be drinking it together at the beach that night.

Getting drunk became a common thing for me, and I would pound beers until I became incredibly intoxicated. I would black out a lot and do extremely crazy and destructive things. One night my friends and I were really hammered and sitting in a McDonalds in Manhattan. The place was very crowed and loud. We were happily eating our food, and the table was full of drinks, hamburgers, and fries. I don't know what came over me, but I suddenly screamed as loud as I could and cleared everything off the table in one full swipe of my arm. The whole restaurant went silent as everybody stared at me. Ethan said we better get out of there, so we left.

Alcohol was a good cure for my shyness, and I had better success with the fairer sex. One night Ethan, Ben, and I were cruising Hylan Boulevard with our friend Frank. We pulled up to a group of three cute girls in their Catholic school uniforms. "Getting nervous?" Frank teased me. But I had liquid courage going for me, so I was able to talk to the girls, and they piled into the car with us. The car was now packed with people, and the girls sat on our laps. From there we went back to Frank's house because his parents were away for the weekend.

I became the drunk ringleader and asked the girls who they wanted to hook up with. One wanted Ben, so I took her hand and put it in Ben's, and they went down to a bedroom. Then Ethan picked another girl, and they went off together as well. I asked the last girl if she wanted to be with me, but she said she wanted to be with Ethan. I told her that Ethan was already taken but that I would love to be with her. She agreed, and we went down to Frank's parents' bedroom. She was really pretty with dark hair and brown eyes and a very cute body.

We made out for a long time and went to second base, so the night was very good. I probably should have gotten her number, but I guess I was too drunk to think that clearly. Still, it was a very good night for all of us, though maybe not for Frank.

During my junior year, I decided to take some time off. I didn't go to school for three months and fooled my parents by hiding out in the garage until they both had left for work. I used these days to hang out and play music and read and get a well-deserved rest.

During one of these days, I was playing baseball with Ethan and Ben. Ethan, who threw very hard, was pitching to me. I mistimed it and tried to catch the baseball in the webbing of my glove, but the ball hit me directly in the nose. I bled so much that my white T-shirt was completely dyed red in the front. It really hurt, and Ben and Ethan could not stop laughing. Since we were all cutting out, I did not go to the doctor, but later an examination showed I had clearly broken my nose. There still is a small bump there today.

After my three months of self-imposed exile was over, I returned to school and was greeted by many friends in the hallways with shouts of "Welcome back, Dave!" and "How's Butch, Dave?" Of course, my grades that term reflected my vacation status, and with a 45 GPA, I had failed all my classes.

I asked out a girl from the supermarket where I worked because she was always winking at me and she was cute. She accepted, and we went out for Chinese food and then back to her house to hang out. Her friend was there with her boyfriend, and they were making out furiously. I felt awkward and did not try to kiss her. At the end of the date, she told me she was getting back with her old boyfriend. So that was that.

On my eighteenth birthday, I was hanging out with my good friend Vincent, and we were drinking a lot at a place called the mansion, which was really some rich guy's house in the Saint George part of the island. We got pretty hammered, and I met a girl named Karen, who I knew from my new job working at a catering hall in the kitchen. Karen was a waitress there.

After a few hours, we took Butch and went back to Vincent's house. Karen came with us. We were hanging in Vincent's bedroom drinking Jack Daniels and getting even more intoxicated. By early morning it started to snow, and Karen said she had to go home. I told her I would drive her, and we departed Vincent's house together. And yes, I know I was driving drunk, which I did all the time, to my horror now. I can't believe I never got into an accident.

I was driving slowly up Victory Boulevard toward Karen's apartment building when I said to her, "Wow, you're really drunk. Should I take advantage of you?"

"Do you want to?" she asked.

I replied, "Yes, definitely." She lunged across the seat and started making out with me furiously. I stopped the car in the middle of the road, and we kept making out, then she told me to go park somewhere.

I went back to Vincent's block, which was a dead-end street, and parked where no one would be watching. She immediately pulled open my pants and went down on me. I was so drunk, I barely even felt it. Soon we both stripped off our clothes and got into the back seat. I asked her if I should use a condom, which I had in my glove box, but she said it was not necessary.

I should point out that at this time I was a virgin, and this was shaping up as my first-time having sex. She knew I was inexperienced and took the lead. I remember at one point I was lying down and looking out the window, watching the snow fall and thinking, *I can't believe this is finally happening.* After we got dressed and I took her home, she wrote her name and number in eyeliner on a piece of paper and told me she wanted to fuck me on her silk sheets.

I drove back to Vincent's house where I was sleeping over and told him I had just gotten laid. He was happy for me that I had finally lost my virginity. I was happy that night too, but things started to change when I sobered up.

I began to have mixed emotions about it and eventually just felt terrible and confused. I had wanted my first time to be with somebody I loved and not just a drunken encounter. Karen was a very nice girl, as well as pretty and funny, but I was not in love with her. I was twisted emotionally by the whole thing. I wanted my first time to me like my first kiss with somebody I loved and who was special to me. I wanted it to be with a serious girlfriend. On the other hand, I was glad to lose the stigma of being a virgin. I never called her, even though I knew it was a sure thing.

Back at work on a weekend, Karen approached me in the kitchen and said, "You hate me, don't you?"

"I don't hate you, Karen," I replied.

"No, you hate me." she exclaimed. And she was right. I hated her and myself and the whole damn thing. It twisted me up inside because I knew I could never get that night back and had it been special like I'd wanted.

In the summers during the last two years of high school, I worked full time with a landscaping company. I was not mowing lawns or anything like that. My boss was a landscaping engineer, and we turned big backyards full of dirt into veritable oases. We would bring in gazebos and build beautiful stone walls and plant many wonderful trees and gardens. It was really amazing what we did.

My boss, Dom, was a cool guy who I loved. He was fun and funny and smart and used to tell us all, "We can do anything!" Sometimes he and I would sit in his truck and have long conversations, and he told me once that he liked to hang out with me because he learned stuff. The work was physical and hard but I loved it, and at that young age, the hot summers did not bother me.

I worked there with Ethan and some friends from the baseball team. One of them, an Italian guy who was a boxer and who got all the girls, became terrified when I told him I was an atheist. He was sure I was going to be struck by lightning, and he would not stand next to me for a while. Unfortunately, he died way too young of cancer years later.

One night during senior year, Frank, Ethan, Ben, and I were cruising in Butch. We were very drunk and having a great time. Frank was in the seat next to me, and Ethan and Ben were in the back. For some reason Ben decided to give me wet willies while I was driving. If you don't know what a wet willy is, it's wetting your fingers and sticking them in someone's ear. I screamed at him a few times, but he wouldn't stop. I turned around with the car still going down the road and took a swing at him. Being six foot five and strong, Ben grabbed my wrists and would not let me go.

I don't know who was steering the speeding car at that point; I just assumed Frank took the wheel. Ben and I continued to scream at each other, and he told me I better not hit him. He was holding my wrists anyway, and I could not break free. Eventually I relented and got back behind the wheel. We all calmed down with some music through Butch's kicking sound system that I had installed.

Senior year was going okay. I knew I had to go to class a lot more and actually do some work in order to get enough credits to graduate. I had an algebra and trigonometry class, and I just hated math. We had a great and hilarious teacher named Mr. Greenbaum. He was Jewish and quirky and funny, and he was a very nice man as well. Because I was such a bad student previously in math, I really disliked it. I sat with Ethan and another friend of ours in the back of the class, making jokes and being loud all the time and driving the teacher crazy. We were the only three seniors in the class; everyone else was younger and more serious.

He called us the three musketeers and teased that we would see him in summer school. Mr. Greenbaum was trying to teach the class, and the three of us were constantly interrupting him and mocking him. It was all in good fun, though, as we sincerely all liked one another.

Toward the end of the year, I approached Mr. Greenbaum after class and talked to him seriously. I asked if he could please pass me with a 65 so that I could graduate with my class. My other marks were fine; it was just this class holding me back. He said that I had about a 42 percent average on all the tests for the year but that if I passed the upcoming Regents exam, he would pass me and let me graduate. I was kind of bummed because I knew I could not pass that exam, and I really did not want to go to summer school.

The day of the regents came, and I showed up at Wagner High School prepared to go down in flames. When I got to the door, I read the sign on it, and to my surprise I had the date wrong. The exam was not until the next day. I was pissed off at first but then said to myself, *well, I got a whole day to study, so maybe I'll try.* I drove Butch to the bookstore in the mall and bought the Barron's study guide for this math Regents exam.

When I got home at about noon, I sat down to study. I was really intense about it and studied for twelve hours straight before going to bed late that night. The next day I got up early and took the regents. Back in class Mr. Greenbaum could not believe it—I had gotten a 66 percent, enabling him to keep his word and pass me so that I could graduate on time and move on with my life. I had learned the whole years' worth of work in one day, and I was surprised I actually passed. Ethan was not so lucky and had to go to summer school.

Chapter 7

BUTCH

After high school I started to smoke pot with my friends who had been smoking it for years. I was not very good at it and did not get high for months until Frank took me aside in his car at an Yngwie Malmsteen concert and taught me the right way to inhale so that I could "stop wasting everybody's weed!" I got so stoned, I was practically hallucinating, and I was freaking out at the concert. I believed everybody was chanting at me— "Dave! Dave! Dave!" I was so paranoid, I thought I was going to get jumped.

I became a regular pot smoker soon after and loved to drive around stoned in my car and listen to music at top volume. I had installed glass-pack mufflers and dual exhaust. The car was so loud now that I am sure my neighbors wanted to kill me.

On one occasion my friend Vince and I were completely stoned and driving Butch to Brother's Pizza on Port Richmond Avenue. Brothers was our favorite pizzeria. They were open until two in the morning, so we were always stopping there late. When we got there that night, there was a bunch of tough-looking guys hanging out next to their truck. In my inebriated condition, I could not judge things well. I drove too close to their truck and sideswiped them.

They started screaming at us and jumped into their now scratched-up truck as we got the hell out of there. The chase was on, and it was a wild one. They pursued us for miles around Staten Island but could not overtake Butch and his 350 engine, plus my modifications. Eventually we went off-road and I had no idea where the hell we were. We somehow got onto the train tracks, and I was driving at top speed directly stuck to the tracks. With a huge bump, I jumped the car back over the tracks and into the dirt, where we were free again. The men who were chasing us had given up, and I guess we had avoided a probable beating.

People always wanted to race me, and sometimes strangers would show up and challenge me to a quarter mile drag race. One time a kid I barely knew from the neighborhood rang my bell and asked me to race. I don't remember what kind of car he had, but it was some souped-up jalopy. We raced down the service road from the light, and Butch and I beat him easily.

The spring after my high school graduation, I enrolled in the community college nearby. I was driving down Ocean Terrace to get to my class, blasting Metallica on my huge car speakers and amplified system, when I came upon a car going very slowly in front of me, which pissed me off. Being a nineteen-year-old kid, I did not have the patience I do today. In typical young Dave fashion, I drove right up on his ass and not only blasted the music but also leaned on the horn for the whole ten minutes I was following him.

When we got to the college entrance, he went through it too but turned into the staff parking lot, and I found a spot in the lot reserved for students. It was the first day of classes, so I was annoyed that some stupid old man was going to make me late. When I got to the class, the professor was sweating and partially hyperventilating with anxiety as he told us that he had almost been killed and that some maniac had chased him all the way down the hill. I knew it was me, and I slunk down in my seat hoping not to be recognized. Luckily, he had not identified me from his rearview mirror, and I was saved from his anger and other consequences.

One day as I was leaving school, I started up Butch's engine, and this annoying kid who nobody liked jumped on the hood of my car. He was a big six-foot two Indian dude, and he decided to take a belly flop and lie down on my hood with his stupid face grinning at me through the windshield.

I thought, *oh, he wants to play*. I put the car into drive and slammed my foot onto the accelerator. Down the street we went, going faster and faster, but he was holding on tight. I slammed on the brakes, and he could not hold on anymore and went flying off into the street. After a good laugh, I drove off. Over the next few days, people came up to me to say they'd heard I'd run over the big Indian, and they congratulated me. Someone said he was going to sue me, but he wasn't really hurt, so nothing else happened. I guess that's the last time he'd be jumping on any cars.

In my mind I thought Butch was the spirit of my car. I imagined he was a big Black angel who was watching over me. My mother always said I had a guardian angel, and I thought this angel who I called Butch was always protecting me. In fact, I never had any type of accident in the car, even though I frequently drove drunk or stoned or on LSD or lots of other drugs. It did seem like a miracle that I was never hurt and that I did not hurt anybody else in the reckless driving of my youth.

At one point I installed a CB radio I bought from RadioShack. It had an outlet for a PA speaker, so I bought and installed that too. I ran the wires through a hole I drilled in the fire wall. I had so much fun scaring and screaming at people on the street with the PA speaker turned up full blast.

One time I was visiting a friend in New Jersey. We went to a party, and everyone was drunk and stoned. Another guy and I decided to go to the diner on Route 17 and get some food. As I drove way too fast down the block, I was screaming at the top of my lungs through the PA system and having a wonderful time.

I was so drunk that I was falling over in our booth at the diner, and the other kid was being really obnoxious to the waitress. We decided to leave, and within seconds of turning the engine on, we were surrounded by four cop cars. They encircled the vehicle and shined flashlights in my eyes and asked if I was doing cocaine. I told them I had just had a beer or two, but I knew I was in for a DWI for real.

Just then another cop recognized my friend as the brother of a guy who worked with them at the police station. They talked to him nicely, and they told us to get a ride home and that they would let us off. My other friend quickly showed up and drove us home. That stroke of luck saved me from losing my license and possibly going to jail as well. Butch was watching over us again.

On another occasion I was driving stoned with Ethan and Ben to the 7-Eleven for some snacks. I was minding my own business when a 1979 Camaro came up the street. This guy must have thought he owned the road because he'd centered himself in the middle of it and was coming right toward us.

I guess he wants to play chicken, I thought. I screamed out to nobody in particular, "We are going through this motherfucker!" I pointed Butch dead down the middle of the road straight into the oncoming Camaro and floored it as the engine roared. Ethan and Ben screamed at me, but I was not giving up. As we went faster and faster toward a head-on collision, the Camaro driver turned out of way at the last second. Butch had won again.

For some reason I felt untouchable in that car, and I did many other crazy things. One of the stupidest was going to the top of my block, which had two parts, and floor the motor. With the needle on the speedometer pinned at 120 mph, I would fly through the stop sign without slowing down at all. This gave me such a rush. It was like a drug or something.

I loved that car like a son for some strange reason, but one day while cruising after getting some Kentucky Fried Chicken, there was a huge bang from the engine, and the motor died right there. I could not afford to rebuild or replace the engine, so I had the car towed to my backyard in Staten Island, and there he sat for the next twenty years.

Because of my manic depression, I was never well enough to work full time to pay for the rebuild, and I wanted to use the same numbers matching engine. Many times, over the years, men rang my doorbell and tried to buy it from me, but I never had the heart to sell him. It was such a dream to me to be able to fully restore Butch one day, but unfortunately it never happened.

I had a wonderful girlfriend in my late twenties who offered to pay for the rebuild, but I knew it was just too much money, and I did not want her to spend it. Years after that, while I was working teaching piano and guitar, I was able to save enough to buy another Oldsmobile Cutlass S on eBay from an older couple in California. The car was absolutely pristine, like it had just come from the factory.

The car was cameo white with gold pinstriping. It was beautiful and had been meticulously kept by the previous owner, who'd bought it new in 1969. I liked the car and enjoyed it. I tried to keep it nice, but even under a car cover, the three New York winters it experienced started to take their toll in small ways. I was a much different person then; I was sober and drove it very carefully and safely.

Even though I enjoyed my classic car, it was not Butch, and I could never replace the love I had for my original Cutlass. After three years of cruising, I decided it would be best to sell it. A couple from South Carolina bought it for exactly what I'd paid for it. They had fond memories of a similar car they'd had when they'd first started dating. I was happy it was going to a good home, and I knew it would be taken care of.

I only had Butch up and running for about four years all told before he died, but that car has haunted my dreams for a lifetime. I was always sad that it was my disability that made it impossible for me to restore my first car. While all my friends were making great money and getting married and having kids, I spent my adult life never able to work enough to afford this luxury. I just hope that the person who bought him restored the car to perfect condition, which was always my dream.

Chapter 8

LSD

(1989)

I did very well during my first term at the College of Staten Island and was approved for a transfer to the State University of New York at Buffalo. My best friend, Frank, was going to attend there that coming fall. We decided to be roommates. I was doing more drugs at this time, specifically cocaine on the weekends. Most of my cocaine binges were with Ethan, and we would hang out at strip bars a lot and snort the white powder in the bathroom.

I smoked a lot of pot as well, and my drinking was mostly binging on the weekend with my cocaine use. Still, I was functioning well and had a high GPA at the college, which is what allowed me to transfer to SUNY Buffalo, a much better school. It was an eight-hour car ride up the New York State Thruway. I've always loved the winters, so I was not put off by the prospect of the frigid and snowy Buffalo winters.

I wanted to major in astronomy, as it had been my dream since childhood to be a scientist and study the stars. I wanted to get some of my required courses in, so I enrolled in physics, calculus, and chemistry. What I did not realize at the time was that I had been a poor math student for many years and was not prepared for these high-level courses. After about a month, I was hit in the face with the fact that there was no way in hell I could pass these classes.

I became depressed when I realized my dream of being a scientist was next to impossible. I turned to drugs to squash these feelings of failure. I started smoking pot every day, all day, and my alcohol and cocaine use increased as well. I stopped going to class and spent my time getting high and hanging out with my friends.

The summer of 1989 came, and I knew I would have to change my major at Buffalo when I went there in the fall. I thought I would do a philosophy degree with a minor in music. That summer was a turning point for me, as I began a season-long spree of tripping on LSD and magic mushrooms.

I did my first acid trip with a bunch of friends at my house while my parents were gone for the weekend. I looked at the little tab of acid with the unicorn on it, not realizing that my life would be changed forever by this tiny piece of acid-soaked paper. The drug started to kick in and everything looked strange. I was staring at a landscape painting my cousin had done, and it came alive.

I saw the water moving and heard the bubbling brook make splashing sounds. The trees were lit up, and it seemed like I was staring into a portal. We were all smoking a ton of weed at the same time, and after peaking at about the two-hour mark, we were still getting higher and higher. It lasted about twelve hours. We were smoking out of a homemade gravity bong, and the smoke was so thick that it made the kitchen ceiling black.

The next weekend we all tripped out again, this time at Silver Lake Park. After dropping the acid before we left for the park, we put magic mushrooms on some hot pizza, as they did not taste so great, and smoked marijuana continuously.

I was tripping hard and lying barefoot on the ground, looking up at a tree. In my mind, the tree and the sky merged. I forgot my name or who I was and simply became one with the universe. Everything was one. I knew it now; I could see and feel it. Everything was changing for me and my perceptions.

Having been an atheist since my bar mitzvah at thirteen, I was not prepared for the way I would change immensely. It was not that I saw God or had some angelic vision; it was more of a huge change in my perception of reality. I realized that what I was seeing with my eyes and my other senses was not the only reality. I was aware of just a small piece of reality and of the small segment of the electromagnetic spectrum. Everything was relative to my observations. What I thought was physical reality was just energy, and my perception of that was completely subjective, maybe even random.

This changed everything for me as I did more and more acid over the summer and became a spiritual seeker and a believer in something more than just plain matter. I knew now that it was energy and that we were all connected at some deep level. Instead of reading books on science, I turned to works on spirituality and religion, and my curiosity was intense. I wanted to learn everything about God and the unseen world. The first book I read completely changed my life. It was called *Autobiography of a Yogi* by Paramahansa Yogananda. It opened me up to things I had never even heard of—Eastern thought and karma and reincarnation and just amazing miraculous things. My knowledge was expanding to places I had never been. I wanted to go to India and find a guru and meditate for hours. I wanted to be a yogi myself one day and learn from spiritual masters. I started to pray for wisdom, as I had done in my childhood. I knew I had one goal in life and that was enlightenment.

One night I was hanging out by Wagner High School with a bunch of guys I knew from school, and I had three tabs of acid in my wallet. I asked if anyone wanted to trip with me, but nobody seemed to be in the mood. Then one blond-haired guy who was really just an acquaintance said he was down to trip out that night.

We each did one and a half of the tabs, and we got into my old Monte Carlo and headed off into the night. Butch had broken down by then, and my cousin had given me the old beat-up Monte as a gift. We headed up the hill to Wagner College, which had a beautiful scenic overlook from which to watch the ocean as well as lots of parking spaces in the lot. I stopped at the security gate and just gave them a wave as if I belonged there, and they let us in.

We sat in the car for a while with the moonroof open, and the acid started to kick in. We got on top of the hood of the old car with our backs to the front widow and watched the beautiful bay and clear summer night through the LSD-induced vision. That night was so peaceful and magical. We hardly spoke at all, but we seemed to share an almost nonverbal communication, almost like telepathy. We felt at one with all of creation and the universe. Words were not necessary. We stayed there all night and into the morning and then I drove him home and went back to my house to sleep. I never saw the dude again, but I'll always have the great memory of our trip.

Not every trip that summer was so spiritual. One evening I was hanging out with old friends Carter and James, tripping on acid at James's house and downing slug after slug off a bottle of Jack Daniels, which gave me a really strange sensation as it passed down my throat. It made my whole body warm and tingly. The three of us had been friends since elementary school, and we always had hilarious times together. Carter and James were best friends and lived across the street from each other.

After a long night of tripping and drinking, James looked at Carter and then at me and threw up all over me. I screamed at the top of my lungs and ripped off all my clothes. I left immediately and ran down the block to my house, naked except for my underwear. I cut through the backyard of the house directly behind mine, and with my bare feet I ran over a huge thornbush. The sensation of the thorns cutting into my feet while on acid was really weird and painful.

Once safely in my house, I put on new clothes, grabbed my car keys, and drove back to James's house. There we continued to trip out and have fun. A few years down the line, James died from his longtime crack addiction.

On another weekend that summer, Frank and I and a bunch of our friends were tripping out on acid at his house. As usual, his parents were gone for the weekend, so we liked to party there. It was a beautiful home in a rich neighborhood overlooking the water. I stared at the curtains in the living room for a long time, and they kept changing shape. I saw different faces in them, and it was completely engrossing as the curtains came to life.

We all were smoking massive amounts of marijuana, and at one point Frank dropped a small half joint over the deck and into the garden below. Frank was so wasted and tripping out that he got paranoid his father would come home and find the joint and know we had been partying in his house. He spent the next three hours on his hands and knees in the overgrown garden looking for the half joint. We all thought this was quite hysterical and stood at the front of the terrace making fun of him and laughing the whole time.

After my summer of acid, I had completely transformed as a human being in many ways. On the one hand, I had become an ardent spiritual seeker and devoted my whole life to God, but on the other hand, my brain was permanently damaged and I became bipolar. By the end of that summer, I did not need the acid to hallucinate anymore. I was doing just fine hallucinating by myself. Everything living had a glow to it. I could see auras, and it seemed like lights were shining from everyone's eyes. I stopped sleeping and barely ate and became very thin. I had manic energy, and my mind was racing at a hundred miles an hour. By my own hand, I had unleashed the demon that was bipolar disorder. I later read many books that cited scientific proof that LSD can bring on manic depression.

It also started a long cycle of SAD, or seasonal affective disorder, where I would become manic every spring and summer and greatly depressed every fall and winter. This continued for decades. I would experience horrible tactile hallucinations, where I would actually feel things in my head that would cause me great physical pain, as if someone were stabbing me in the brain.

LSD might have saved my soul, but in the process, it destroyed my life. I never would be able to work a full-time job, never be able to support myself, and never be able to live even a quasi-normal life again without huge amounts of medications that had horrible side effects and consequences of their own. I was now a truly disabled person, and my adult life had just begun.

Chapter 9

STATE UNIVERSITY OF NEW YORK AT BUFFALO

(1990)

Frank and I were driving to the dorms at SUNY Buffalo from Staten Island. Besides being in my first ever full-blown manic episode, I had filled a large canteen with vodka and orange juice for the eight-hour ride. Frank and I were smoking pot the whole way there, besides me getting completely drunk as well.

About an hour from the school, we noticed that a car had been following us for a long time. Frank kept insisting it was a cop, but I just laughed at him and said he was paranoid. After a good half hour of this, the sirens went on and the lights started flashing; it was indeed a cop.

Frank had become a drug dealer a few years before, and he had about a pound of marijuana hidden in the console of his 1979 Camaro.

I tried to throw a roach we were smoking out the window, but it blew back into the car and we could not find it. The cops, of course, had no trouble locating it, and they took me out of the Camaro and put me in the police car. I was so drunk that I was laughing hysterically and chatting amiably with the other cop in the cruiser. After a good twenty minutes of this, they actually let us go. Most likely because Frank was not drinking at all, and they never found the huge amount of weed he had hidden in the car.

At the college we shared a large dorm room with two other roommates who seemed nice, if a little on the nerdy side. We went to the Salvation Army and purchased a small couch and television and set up the room a little bit. I cashed in some bonds I had left over from my bar mitzvah and bought a Crate keyboard amplifier and microphone to go with my small Casio keyboard. One of the first things I did there was audition for the music program to minor in piano performance. I went into a big room with a grand piano and played a piece by Mozart and one by Beethoven. I had learned these in the few months I had spent with a teacher in my junior year of high school.

I was never a classical pianist. I was only a self-taught rock piano player, but I had hoped I would get in and learn classical piano. There were a bunch of professors there, and after I played the two pieces, one professor said, "I think I know what we have here." A few days later, they posted the names of the people who had gotten into the program, but my name was not on it. I was very disappointed and upset, and I took the list off the door and ripped it up.

One day a lot of people were hanging out in the dorm room, and I met a girl named Maya. She was so beautiful, with long blonde hair and sparkling green eyes, that I instantly fell in love with her. She seemed to like me as well, and she stayed near me the whole time, but I was too shy to ask for her phone number.

I found a piano in one of the lounges at the dorms, and I was playing and singing the entire album *The Wall* by Pink Floyd when a dude with blond hair walked in and we started talking. He was very into classic rock like I am, and Arron was to become my best friend in Buffalo. Arron was on the wrestling team and liked to drink and party as much as me. For the whole term, we got drunk and high as much as humanly possible.

Frank, meanwhile, had decided to join a fraternity and was pledging for the Sammys, the most notorious fraternity on campus. I was completely against it simply because I don't believe in hazing and think it's juvenile and barbaric. One time one of his fraternity brothers was throwing things at him, and I got pissed and confronted the brother and was about to get physical with him.

Frank asked me not to interfere and told the brother that I just didn't understand, but I do not like people messing with my friends. Even though Frank would spend most of his time with the Sammys and was never at the dorm much, I did not begrudge him for not staying with me, as I had my own life to live too.

One evening I was sitting in my dorm room blasting the Doors music on my stereo when I heard a faint knock through the loud music. I put it on pause and opened the door to see a gorgeous redhead standing there. She told me she loved the Doors, and I invited her in. We sat on the couch and talked for a few minutes before I started kissing her, and we made out for a while. She said she was shy and I was too, but I guess I was in an inspired mood and just went for it.

We started dating and hanging out. She was a very sweet and loving person. The only problem was that she told me she was waiting for marriage to have sex, so we never got past second base. It was really nice, though, to have someone to kiss and cuddle with, and I liked her a lot.

I was still high most of the time, and by the third week, I stopped going to classes altogether. I got into a pattern of sleeping during the day and staying up all night watching television. Arron came over almost every night, and we watched *The David Letterman Show*, which we loved.

We would order at least a case of beer most nights and drink it until we were completely soused.

Very soon the nice weather disappeared, and it started snowing every day. This was when my first real clinical depression and the onset of my seasonal affective disorder as part of my manic depression started. Instead of being hyper and manic, I became deeply depressed. I had never known depression like this, and I thought of suicide all the time. There was a lake in front of the dorms, and I used to look at it and think of drowning myself.

My friend Nancy persuaded me to go to a party at her dorm. All the rooms in that hallway were serving different kinds of liquor and beer. I got completely drunk and was making out with a girl in one of the rooms. I got up to get another beer, and the resident adviser got into my face about something. I had a quick temper when I was drunk, and I immediately attacked him physically.

I went crazy, hitting, biting, kicking, and screaming at him. Public safety was called and had to pull me off the guy. It took about six cops to hold me down as I screamed at the top of my lungs about how I was going to get him and kill him as soon as they released me. The cops said I better calm down or they would take me to jail. "Let's go to jail, motherfuckers!" I screamed. They cuffed me and put me into a patrol car.

I was eventually brought before the judge, who immediately said, "You look like trouble."

"I am trouble!" I yelled back at him. I spent the night in the drunk tank singing blues songs the whole time. In the morning the cops laughed and said they liked the floor show.

I was charged with four different offenses and given a court date. A female friend of Arron's told me her uncle was a lawyer, and my parents hired him to get me out of trouble. After borrowing a suit from Arron, I appeared in court and was made to pay a $500 fine. Because this was my first offense, he let me off easy.

My parents paid the lawyer $800 to seal the records because it was my first offense and because I was so young. Unfortunately, he took the money and never filled the paperwork, which would prove disastrous further down the line.

When I came home from court, I was embarrassed and now even deeper into my depression. I never called the girl I'd been seeing, thinking she probably did not want to hang out anymore.

One day a girl I knew, Nancy tried to introduce me to a friend of hers. I was so shy and stoned that I could not even look her in the eyes and just stared at my feet instead, saying nothing. Nancy had to put her hand under my chin and lift my head up to look at the girl, but I was still too shy to talk.

My depression and constant use of marijuana made me deeply paranoid most of the time, and I avoided people in the hallways. I was afraid to talk to anyone and felt like I was surrounded in the dorms. I completely hated my time there. I went out only to get food or drinks. During the day I slept and hid from the outside world.

When Arron and I got drunk, the story changed dramatically, though, as I am capable of really outrageous behavior. One night we got trashed and took some mescaline. Arron and I went on a drunken destructive craze throughout the buildings. We trashed whole classrooms and hallways, ripping down bulletin boards and anything else that was not bolted down.

We then got ahold of a crowbar and went from kitchen to kitchen, prying open locked refrigerators and stealing all kinds of food. We brought our haul to my kitchen and cooked a huge feast. We ate like kings that night. Two stupid drunken kings.

I ran into Maya a few times during the semester, and although she still flirted with me and made it obvious, she liked me too, I was still too shy to ask her out. Then one day I decided to overcome my fears and go for it. Maya lived on another campus downtown, so I took a bus and gathered my courage to go for my dream girl.

The campus was a long way away, but I made it without getting lost and found her dorm room. The door was open, and she stood there looking so absolutely beautiful. The problem was, she was surrounded by about eight guys who were busy talking to her. I knew this was my last chance. I had come all that way, but I was too intimated to try to talk to her among such a big crowd.

I walked away without her even seeing me and got back on the bus across town. For some reason Maya has haunted me all these years later. I always thought that maybe if we had gone out, everything would be different. Maybe she could have seen that I was so sick and depressed and gotten me the help I needed. Maybe I would have gotten off drugs and alcohol if I'd had someone to live for. I thought I would have married her and had children one day, such was my love for this young woman. I guess we will never know. It was the last time I would see her.

With a 0.0 GPA and deeply depressed and drug addicted, my parents wanted to know if I was going to come back for the second term. I hated to be a failure, but I knew I hated school even more. Living in the dorms was like hell for me, and I was always stoned, depressed, and paranoid. One night Arron and I had gotten particularly drunk when I decided to pull a fire alarm for the second time that semester. The first time the whole building had to evacuate in the middle of the night, and I hid in my room. They knew it was me, but I denied it so much that they left me alone.

On another night, though, I did the same stupid thing in my drunken haze, and Arron got blamed for it. I was going home in a few days, and Arron asked me to confess and tell them I had pulled it and not him. I was so paranoid that I would go to jail this time that I did not say anything and let Arron take the fall. He was transferred to another dorm across campus. I have felt tremendous guilt for this cowardly action my whole life. I had let down a good friend and myself and essentially ended our friendship. I had borne false witness against a friend, and this has really hurt me to my core for many years. I had failed yet again.

My father came up soon after, and we loaded my things into his car. We started the long drive back to Staten Island, but the ride was mostly silent. I was lost in my depressive thoughts, and my dad was never a big talker anyway. My mother later said she knew I would never make it when I left, as I was so mentally ill after the summer of LSD. I did not realize it at the time. Mental illness is a very strange thing. Many times, when you are manic, you are the last one to know, and I thought everyone else was crazy.

That term I had spoken to my cousins in New Jersey. Their friend Tiffany—the girl who gave me my first French kiss—was visiting from Florida, and they said I could spend some time with them and her. This had given me such hope and anticipation. I knew it would be a sex-filled time with a girl I was crazy about. And she was extremely hot.

Unfortunately, my parents would not let me go because of the troubles I'd had at school. My time with the beautiful Tiffany was never going to happen. This did not help my depression either, and I spent my time on the couch smoking pot all day and watching television. I had never experienced this feeling before. I had gotten sad or low in my life, but this was something much, much darker. My despair was universal, and all my thoughts were of failure and suicide.

I was in the first of many clinical depressions that I would experience in my life, and my mind tormented me endlessly. All I thought was that my life was over at twenty. I had failed at school. I had failed with women. I had failed at everything. I thought it was all over, so I decided to just end it and kill myself.

I thought of all different ways in which I could do it, and I finally decided that gas was the best. One day when my parents were not home, I blew out the pilot light in the stove and turned on the oven full blast. I thought for sure that I could inhale so much gas that I would be overcome and die, finally ending my misery. The gas was steadily coming out of the oven, and I crawled in to the best of my ability. I stayed in there for a long time, but I did not die. I was pissed off about it but never told a soul.

The crazy thing is that your mind can be so sick in depression that you cannot see reality at all. I was only twenty, but I thought I had no future and no hope. I could see only the negative in everything. I have been through so much in the thirty-five years since. I have had so many wonderful times with friends, family, and lovers and just great experiences. Of course, there have many horrible times as well, but what a tragedy it would have been for those who loved me if I had been successful in my suicide attempt.

My poor mother and father would never have gotten over it. There is nothing worse than losing a child, and that kind of pain would have haunted them forever. For my sisters and the rest of my family, I would have been a tragic memory all their lives. I would never have gotten to see my wonderful nieces and nephews and meet my brother-in-law. I would have missed out on so much learning and love and fun.

Yes, I have had extremely difficult times since then, but I would not trade it to have killed myself that day. I have grown spiritually because of my experiences and have become more of the person I wanted to be. Life is so precious, and it hurts me so much now when I hear that someone has taken their own life. I have known people who have committed suicide, and I always wonder if I could have helped or tried talking to them.

Chapter 10

MANIC FLIGHT TO FLORIDA

(1991)

I stayed depressed for many months until the spring, when the season started to affect my mood. I lost my depression but became quite manic. I was getting thinner and thinner and was down to 121 pounds. At this point my mind was racing, and I was not sleeping and hardly eating. I was still smoking pot continuously, and I had all kinds of wild ideas and plans.

My parents had me see a psychiatrist, who said he was going to put me on medication. This really scared me, as I had never been on psych meds before. I thought he was trying to control me, and it made me extremely paranoid. I decided to escape to Florida by train, and I bought a ticket on Amtrak for as far as I could afford, which was to Washington, DC.

In Washington, I stayed on the train all the way to Florida, even though I did not have a ticket. Well into the state of Florida, they started checking tickets as we approached a town. I knew I could get in trouble and possibly arrested for being a stowaway, so as the train slowed, I took my knapsack and jumped off and onto the grass, where I rolled a few times but was unhurt.

Soon I made my way to Daytona Beach, where I slept on the beach and lived on handouts. The beach was beautiful, and I liked the peace of sleeping there. It was a different kind of place from any I ever had seen, as cars were allowed on the beach and went down the center of the white sands.

One day I was hanging out by the water when a young man approached and told me he thought I was really hot and wanted me to be his boyfriend. I had my shirt off and was I wading in and out of the beautiful water. As he talked to me, he had an erection and was trying to lure me back to his father's hotel.

He told me his father owned a bunch of hotels, and if I would be his boyfriend, he would set me up in a nice room and provide me with whatever I wanted, including food and money. Being completely straight I was never tempted by this offer. I would rather be homeless than have sex with a man.

I talked to him for a while, though, and asked him what it was about men that he liked. He told me that he liked to feel protected by a man and that it made him feel more secure to be with men. Despite being homeless and penniless, I would never prostitute myself by being with a man. That was just disgusting to me.

There were hotels all along the beach with lots of things going on, including very good musical acts. I spent a lot of time hanging out by the bands and watching them. Some were really good, and I was enjoying myself despite being a thousand miles away from my home, family, and friends in Staten Island.

One night I was sleeping on the beach when a huge Florida insect as big as a bird crawled onto me. I freaked out and ran to the hotel nearest me. I decided I needed to stay there for the night, so I kicked open a door and tried to commandeer a room for myself.

Security found me within minutes, and they give me a warning: "Walk to Miami." But I had other plans. In my mania I did the same thing a few days later and broke into another hotel room on the top floor. This room was occupied, and there were suitcases and clothing everywhere. I decided I would make a speech from the balcony to the people below on the patio around the pool.

I took a blanket and wrapped up the television. My crazy plan was to throw the television into the pool to get people's attention and then make a speech from the balcony. This did not work out, as the hotel security busted in and arrested me right away.

They took me to Volusia County Jail. I was extremely nervous to be in a real jail and not just the Buffalo drunk tank. They booked me on three counts of felony burglary, even though I had not stolen anything or had even planned to take anything. I was not given a lawyer, and I did not see a judge; they just locked me up. I was really scared and did not know what was going to happen to me.

An older inmate took me aside and taught me how to survive in jail. He told me to keep to myself and to try to sleep as much as possible but to never allow anyone to put their hands on me. He told me if I was fucked with, I had to fight and defend myself at all costs because I needed to be feared. He also told me if I used my voice and was loud, I might not have to fight.

At some point the guards took my glasses, and I was basically blind in the jail.

I was really scared being in an actual jail for the first time. I asked a guard if they tortured us in there. He said they do and that they liked to use needles. He was just trying to scare me, but I was worried for real. My mom got in touch with a person of authority within the jail and told them

I was mentally ill and should be put in a hospital. He told my mom, "This is Florida. We don't care if they're crazy. We just lock them up."

They would not give me my glasses, so I got extremely angry and rebellious and decided to flood the cellblock. I stuffed the toilet in my cell with clothing and kept flushing it over and over again. The flood worked so well that the entire cellblock was five inches deep in toilet water. Eventually they came for me, though.

They sent three corrections officers to my cell to stop me. There were two white officers, and in between them was a huge six-foot five Black guy who was holding a big broom. I stood in the back of the cell with my ankles deep in the water and screamed, "Come and get me, motherfuckers!" The charged at me, and the Black dude used the broom handle to hit me in the head more than three times.

They dragged me out of the cell and hog-tied me, meaning they put handcuffs around my ankles and wrists and tied them together around my back with another pair of cuffs. Then they threw me into the wall headfirst for good measure. I continued to yell and curse at them. They stripped me naked, turned off the water in my cell, and left me there with no clothes or a mattress or anything.

After several days they gave me some clothes again, but I still did not have my glasses. One inmate told me he had six male prostitutes, and he wanted me to be number seven. He said he would pay me with drugs or alcohol. This scared the shit out of me, so I politely declined and he did not force the issue.

On another occasion an inmate was sitting on a bench in front of all of us and casually took down his pants and started masturbating. I found it completely horrifying and looked away, but nobody else seemed to mind or think it was unusual. Perhaps they were afraid of him as well.

After seven weeks of this, I finally saw a lawyer appointed by the state. He told me that if I pled no contest to one felony that they would drop the other two counts of burglary, and I would not have to go to prison. I would be on eighteen months of probation, though. I took the deal because I did not want to go to prison. I just wanted to get out.

What I did not realize at the time was that I would forever have a felony conviction on my record at the age of twenty-one. Therefore, for the rest of my life, I could never get a real job, even if I was well enough or qualified for it. I could never work in the school system or get a city job or ever work for a white-collar company. In other words, I could never live a normal life. The only jobs open to a felon are low-class, low-paying jobs, and they are the worst kinds of positions. Even though I would later get a bachelor's degree in sociology and make the dean's list, it did not matter because nobody would hire me.

They had railroaded a mentally ill twenty-one-year-old man into what was basically a lifetime sentence. I should have been charged only with breaking and entering, and I should have been put into a mental hospital, as I was obviously very much mentally ill. To further add salt to the wound, if that lawyer in Buffalo had properly sealed my records like my parents had paid him a lot of money to do, my case in Florida could have been expunged as a first offense.

The only thing I could have done was to go to trial, but I was never willing to do that. With three felony charges, I could have gone to prison for many, many years. I was now trapped in the system for the rest of my life and would never be able to get a job that matched my intelligence or skill set.

I was lucky only in the sense that when I was older, I could teach guitar and piano and start my own business. There I was judged simply on my character, presentation, and musical ability. None of my students or their parents ever knew about my disability or my criminal record. I was also hired to teach piano part time in a music school on Staten Island, and my boss knew nothing about my past. He hired me on the recommendation of my music professor, who was a trusted friend of his.

After finally letting me out of jail, the court sent me to a rooming house for people with mental illness. After being there for only a few days, a group of men came to me for help. They explained that a large Black man had been raping them one by one, and they couldn't stop it from happening. The staff did not seem to care about it. I told them they all should jump him at once and give him a beating so that he would learn his lesson, but they were too scared of him.

The Black dude tried to mess with me as well, but I just yelled at him to fuck off. As I walked away, I heard him say, "He's a hard man, but he has a soft behind." This grossed me out, but at least he did not try to rape me. I spent a few days there, hanging out on the beach and watching the music again.

One night the woman in charge, who did not like me at all, said she was transferring me to room with the dude who was raping people. There was no way I was going to risk being asleep with him in the room with me, so I left and became homeless again.

Within a few days, the cops picked me up and charged me with leaving a rooming house. They put me back in Volusia County Jail for the weekend. My parents got in touch with the people in charge of my case and got my probation transferred back to Staten Island.

My mom and dad picked me up from jail, and we flew from there to Newark airport. I was quite manic on the plane. I smoked cigarettes, even though it was not allowed. I screamed and yelled all kinds of crazy stuff. The pilot came back to my seat and told my parents that if I did not stop smoking and be quiet, they would land the plane before Newark and have me arrested.

My mom pleaded with the pilot that I was mentally ill and to please fly me back all the way to Newark. By some miracle the pilot agreed, and we made the whole flight back north. When we got to the airport, they let me out first. I was greeted by a lot of police and put in handcuffs and taken to Elizabeth General Hospital.

They put me in a room and gave me a shot of tranquilizers. Unfortunately, I had a reaction to the medicine. I freaked out and destroyed the room, throwing the furniture against the glass windows. In minutes a whole team of workers flew into the room and held me down. They four-pointed me to the bed, meaning my hands and feet were chained to the bed so that I could not move.

They gave me more and more shots of Haldol until I finally fell asleep. When I awakened, I was much calmer and felt like I had been asleep for a long time. After a few days there, they transferred me to Marlboro Psychiatric Hospital in New Jersey, a large and notoriously bad state hospital.

Chapter 11

MARLBORO PSYCHIATRIC HOSPITAL

(1991)

Marlboro Psychiatric Hospital was a huge facility with thousands of patients. It was divided into housing residences quaintly called cottages. But this was no vacation home. The cottage I was sent to was a large old building with a huge room on the bottom floor with about one hundred chairs. We were made to sit all day and into the night until bedtime.

There was a dining hall that we were marched to three times a day for food. There were no activities or therapy, even though there were bulletin boards filled with an activity schedule. This was just for show, I guess, because all we could do was sit on the chairs all day long and do nothing.

I was heavily medicated and so tired all the time that all I wanted to do was sleep. I had crashed from my manic episode due to the heavy drugs, and now I was depressed and anxious and just wanted to go home and sleep.

One day I put two chairs together so that I could sleep when some dude started arguing with me about it. Things got really heated, and he punched me in the nose. I started bleeding profusely, and he asked me if I was going to come back at him. I declined the invitation. I was scared and shaking and trying to keep the blood off my new sneakers.

They X-rayed my nose, but it was not broken. They told me he was just paranoid and to stay away from him. I was really scared of him from that point on. Although he could be menacing, he did not punch me again.

A beautiful blonde girl at the hospital kept asking me to be her boyfriend, but I knew she already had a boyfriend because he came to see her all the time. I really liked her, though, and we would sit and talk a lot. I would brush her hair, which I loved doing because it was sensual, but I did not overstep my bounds and kiss her like she wanted me to.

My mother felt really badly that I was there so long and in such a horrible place. One day she called and said she was going to bring my cat, Teddy, for a visit. Teddy was an all-gray cat that I loved dearly. Mom brought him in his carrier, and they allowed me to go out to the car to pet him and play with him. It made me very happy.

After they left my mom called me on the pay phone with some horrible news. Teddy had gotten loose somehow and had run into the woods. I was devastated and could not believe this was happening. If I was depressed before, now I was really despondent. My mom called back in about an hour and said she had gotten some ham from the store and was able to get Teddy back. I was so happy and relieved.

The people at the hospital decided I should go to another cottage that was also for drug rehab. This program was extremely regimented, and it had drug and alcohol groups all day, beginning very early in the morning. I was so tired and overmedicated. I really hated it and asked them to put me back in the cottage I had been in before. They refused and said I had to stay there and go through the program. I decided to take a page out of Gandhi's book and use passive resistance to get their attention.

I refused to go to any programs and would not even get out of bed. I went completely limp, and they had to physically drag me from program to program. I would lie on the floor and not resist. They dragged me up and down stairs and through hallways. After a few days of this, I won and they threw me out. I guess I was more trouble than it was worth.

Back at the original cottage, they put me into an interrogation setting they called the hot seat. All the higher staff and doctors sat around a long table and fired questions at me. It was very intense, and I don't know why they would put a sick person through that. They did not treat me like a sick person but more like a criminal before a jury. Those kinds of tactics were common at Marlboro, and they seemed particularly harsh and unnecessary as I think back on it today. There was no compassion at all.

Believe it or not, there were some fun times at the hospital. Another patient and I used to sit on the floor in the hallways and sing. Some other patients also sometimes got into it. We particularly liked to sing the Canadian national anthem, and we would laugh and laugh.

I made friends with some other patients, and one day this guy smuggled in some opium oil from one of his guests. We had grounds privileges by this time, so we put the opium on our cigarettes and got really happy and mellow. That was a good day for me and my little group of friends.

I had been at Marlboro Psychiatric Hospital for three long months when I was interviewed by one of the doctors. He was looking at his computer and talking to me and then he got up to do something for a minute. I took this moment to look at his computer screen and read what he had written about me. I noticed it said that I was delusional.

I had been very stable and not manic for months, and I did not know until then that this was the reason they were keeping me so long. When he returned, I told him I didn't believe those things anymore, and by some miracle they released me the next day. I could not believe that this was the reason I was held up in the psychiatric hospital for so long.

I was so happy to be going home and to finally be free from this crazy adventure that had started with my manic run to Florida, going to jail, and everything that had happened to me in the past year. Now I was reunited with my family and my cats and my wonderful home in Staten Island. I could sleep in my own bed again and breathe the free air. I was still overmedicated and depressed but not to the point I was before. I was just relieved that it was all over.

Unfortunately, when I got home, I found out that none of my friends wanted anything to do with me anymore. Only Ethan remained my friend and would talk to me or hang out. All my friends from elementary school, junior high, and high school had completely abandoned me. Even one of my best friends from high school had his mother tell me when I called that he went away to Europe for the summer. I knew this was bullshit, but there was nothing I could do. The stigma of mental illness had scared them all away.

At home I crashed hard from my manic episode. It left me very anxious and depressed. My parents insisted I go to a program every day from nine in the morning until two in the afternoon. It was a MICA program, which stands for mentally ill and chemically addicted. I hated it with a huge passion. I had no car and had to take the bus every morning into a bad part of town.

The doctor there refused to put me on antidepressants because he was afraid that I'd become manic. It was some kind of state technicality. They did not want to take the chance. Still, I was tired all the time from the meds and really anxious. I had no social life and spent my days reading, watching television, or playing the piano.

My therapist at the program was terrible. We mostly just stared at each other for the session. He would ask, "What are your issues?"

I replied, "My life sucks." It was all I could think of.

We were in groups all day where we talked about things with the other patients. I found it quite boring and stupid and just wanted to go home and sleep. My life had changed so quickly, going from a rich social life with tons of friends to having no one but Ethan to talk to. And he was very busy with his live-in girlfriend now.

On Fridays we would go to the YMCA and play volleyball, which was the only thing I liked about the program. At least I was not in a state of manic psychosis anymore, but my life was just drudgery.

Chapter 12

MEN GET MOLESTED TOO

I'm going to take a small detour from the narrative of my life to focus on a subject I think is very important. There is an epidemic of sexual abuse in this country that I have been made aware of through interactions with women who were friends or girlfriends, but I wanted to share my story and let readers know that this happens to men as well. Women are not alone.

When I was thirteen, on the night after my bar mitzvah, I was hanging out with an older friend. On a few occasions, he had asked me if I wanted to play rape. I always declined and did not even know what this meant. This particular night he was sleeping over, and he turned the TV to a scrambled channel but on which we could see sex scenes. Of course I was turned on, but I had no idea what was going to happen next.

I was lying under the blanket when I felt his hand touch my private parts. It tingled, and I was already excited from the porn, but I really did not know what was going on. I was never attracted to men in any way. I was always falling in love with girls and dreaming and fantasizing about them. I was and am completely straight and have never had any attraction to boys or had even thought about them.

He continued to touch me, and I did not know what to do. I wasn't intimidated by him in any way and it was not forced, but I was confused as to why it felt good. This was my first sexual experience. He gave me oral sex and asked me to return the favor, which I did not want to do.

There was never any penetration or kissing, and he even said that he was not gay because gay guys kiss. I think I would have punched him in the face if he'd tried to kiss me. He also said he was molesting two young boys, ages seven and nine, who he was babysitting.

The whole experience made me sick and confused and changed me a lot. I no longer believed in God and became an atheist because I could not believe God would let this happen to me. It screwed me up emotionally. It happened again on a couple of other occasions and then finally stopped. I had to work through this in therapy many years later because in some ways I blamed myself and did not even know I had been molested.

Years later when I was in my forties, I was brought to South Beach Psychiatric Center as a patient. I had to see the doctor for a physical, which was standard practice. I was manic and exhausted from being brought there. I was led into the room by an older female nurse and a young female doctor. They had me strip down to my underwear and then the nurse left the room, shutting the door and leaving me alone with the doctor.

She did not examine me at all. She did not listen to my heart or take my blood pressure or do any of the usual things that would happen during a physical examination. She told me she wanted to take a quick peak, and as she said that, she grabbed my boxer shorts and pulled them open to take a long look at my penis. She then said she wanted another quick peak and did the same exact thing—pulling open my boxers to stare at my penis for a while.

I felt extremely uncomfortable and embarrassed. I did not know what to do, so I just stood there. After a few minutes of this, she told me I could go. I silently got dressed as she left the room. She never examined me, never asked me any medical questions, and never did anything except ogle my body. I was extremely humiliated, and when I got up to my room, I complained to the staff about it.

I did not know if this would have any effect, but at about twelve thirty in the morning, a group of upper staff management barged into my room while I was sleeping and started firing questions at me about the incident. I was shocked and alarmed by the intensity of it all. I told them my story, but they did not believe me. At this point I just wanted to go back to sleep and be done with it.

I don't know whatever happened to that doctor, but I thought she should be fired. Being mentally ill, I was very vulnerable and alone in a mental hospital, and this woman used me for her sexual gratification, at least visually. I was in the hospital for months, but thankfully I never saw this doctor again. At the end of my stay, a man wanted me to sign a piece of paper saying I had made the whole thing up, but I refused and told him that what I said was exactly what had happened.

On another occasion I was in jail at Rikers Island for a year, although I had not been convicted of anything. Rikers Island was a terrible place, and lots of bad things happened to the people there. I was taken out of my cellblock one day, and the guards had us all line up against the wall to frisk us and check for weapons, I suppose. One very large Black guard with a beard took me aside and put me against another wall away from the other inmates. He proceeded to grab my penis and balls in his large hands and squeeze them tightly, causing me great pain, especially in my stomach.

I asked to see the doctor and told him what had happened. He was very nice as he examined me and told me I was very lucky I did not have permanent damage. I had pain in my lower abdomen for days, and I complained to the captain about what had occurred. They took it much more seriously than my complaint at South Beach.

The police interviewed me, taking my story down on tape and asking me lots of questions. They were businesslike and serious. The main problem was that I had accused a corrections officer of sexual assault, so now I was vulnerable to attack from him or his friends. In fact, every time I had to leave the cellblock, he and another officer would trail behind me, calling me a faggot and a pussy and trying to get under my skin. My lawyers asked if I wanted to sue Rikers for the incident, but I thought it was very unwise to sue this corrupt facility while I was still there. Anything could and did happen to people, and I did not want something even more dangerous to happen to me. I talked to the police one more time, but I have no idea whatever became of the case. They never told me.

When I was in my early twenties and in Marlboro Psychiatric Hospital, I got an injection of Prolixin every week for the symptoms of bipolar disorder. I became very stable on this medication, and it had few side effects. One day I was in the nurse's office with a few staff around, and the nurse had me drop my pants and underwear to give me the shot in my ass. Instead of giving me the shot, though, she squeezed and kneaded my ass cheeks.

I was very upset about being molested by someone I trusted, and I complained to the staff, but they told me I was making it up. One male staff member said to me, "Why would she do that? You are not a handsome guy."

I replied, "Well, you're an ugly motherfucker yourself." They did nothing about it, but I refused to have any more shots. They had to change my meds to an oral prescription that did not work as well and possibly led me to having another breakdown in the future.

It's amazing the things that can happen to a man or a woman when they are in such vulnerable positions. And these are professional college-educated doctors and nurses acting like this. I've known two women who were raped in the shower by staff members at mental hospitals. This goes on all the time.

In my forties I was living in Staten Island in a government-funded apartment with a roommate. I was quite stable and happy and was once again taking shots of Prolixin every few weeks. This was the miracle med that helped me return to normal stability and mental clarity.

I had a male nurse who was a former cop, and I liked him a lot. We used to talk all the time. One day when he was giving me the injection, he decided to make a comment about my body and said I had gorgeous buttocks. I did not answer him, but it made me feel very uncomfortable. I don't think it's proper etiquette for a doctor or nurse to talk about your body when you are exposed and vulnerable. I did not make a big deal about it, but I include it here because I know that many women have to put up with this kind of treatment. I found it perverse, especially because he was supposedly a straight male like me.

The final story I will tell you is when I was protesting at Zuccotti Park in Manhattan for the Wall Street demonstrations that were taking place. We camped out in the park for several days, but because so many women were being raped, the mayor shut down the demonstrations.

They brought many of us by subway to a church to sleep; it was supposed to be a safe house. We were packed in like sardines in a few large rooms and had sleeping bags or blankets. I was talking to some of my new friends from the demonstrations when a very wild and probably drunk trans woman ran up to me and exposed her breasts. She obviously liked me, but she freaked me out and was quite an unattractive and rude person. Yet she persisted in trying to gain my favor.

I had a bad feeling about the whole thing, and I warned her very seriously that she had better not fuck with me while I was sleeping. I repeated this a few times, but she just laughed and walked away.

A few hours later, I was fast asleep when this trans woman tried to fuck me up the ass. I freaked out and gave her what I called the Patton necktie, a defensive kill move I had invented many years ago in which I jam two fingers into the soft area of the neck beneath the Adam's apple. I'd never had to use it before, but before I let any scumbag rape me, I would rather kill or die trying.

Everything happened very quickly, but I managed to stick my fingers right into her neck, and she became a bloody mess. She ran away as quickly as she could. I have been a piano player my whole life, and my hands are lightning quick, so she was lucky to be alive.

Eventually the people running the protest brought me to a room where the trans woman had been treated and who now had a bloody bandage around her neck. I did not feel sorry for her at all. I said to the now very sober and calm trans person, "I told you do not fuck with me when I was sleeping, and I meant it." They decided it was best that I leave the church. I did but not until I demanded they give me all their tobacco and some rolling papers, which they gladly did.

The explosion of sexual abuse and rape across our nation is rampant, especially for people in vulnerable populations. These are just some of the experiences that I faced as a man. Imagine what women must go through. There is an epidemic of so-called date rape at college campuses, and some schools have had to shut down fraternity parties because of all the drugging and raping of women. This is happening on college campuses, where we are supposed to send our best and brightest. I really have no words to describe how terrible and traumatizing sexual abuse is and what it can do to a person's life. People need to keep their hands to themselves.

Chapter 13

NEW PALTZ, NEW YORK

In this chapter I will talk about the upstate New York town of New Paltz. Just ninety miles north of New York City, this small town has played a huge role in my life. I mention it in many parts of the book, but I wanted to dedicate a single chapter to the place I love so much. The first time I visited it was when I was a teenager and looking into colleges. The State University of New York at New Paltz was on my list as one of the state schools my parents could afford.

It was supposed to be simply a day trip to tour the college and the town, but the night before we left, I had a vision that we would break down and have to stay over. I packed an overnight bag and told my parents, but they just laughed and said I was being silly.

We drove the ninety miles upstate, and I enjoyed looking at the mountains. I had always loved upstate New York since I was a child, and we'd go to a bungalow colony every summer in the Catskills. I wanted to live in the Catskills, and I dreamed about a mountain house on a peaceful lake with deer and beautiful animals all around. I love nature and the peace of it all.

We got to the college and took the tour given to prospective students. They brought us to a dorm room that was painted all in black with lots of weird stuff hanging from the walls and ceilings. They were artists, but at that stage of my development, I did not consider myself an artist or know much about it, and I found it creepy.

The town was quaint, and we had a nice lunch, but as predicted by my vision, the car broke down. The mechanic said we had to wait for a part, and it would not be ready until the next day. It was a telling omen of how big a role the town of New Paltz would play in my life, even though at the time I had no idea at all.

I decided against going to school there and did not even think of the town for many years, until one day in my late twenties a good friend and I were bored on a Sunday, and I suggested we get in the car and go anywhere upstate. With no destination in mind, we headed up the New York State Thruway and enjoyed the scenery and the peace of the mountains. Eventually we came to a sign for exit 18 to New Paltz. For no reason at all, I told my friend to get off there so that we could check the place out.

We did, and it would forever alter my life, as this hippie wonderland cast a spell over me. New Paltz in the 1990s was like a flashback to San Francisco in the 1960s. Everyone wore full hippie regalia, and it was like stepping back in time. I felt like I belonged there and knew I needed to live there one day.

All the shops were full of hippie and spiritual items, and we walked around spellbound. It was so different from our hometown just ninety miles south. The restaurant we ate at was wonderful, and the girls from the college were everywhere and so beautiful and hippied out. When we drove home, I could not stop thinking about the place, and I felt sad that we had to leave at all.

Over the years that followed, I would visit there about once a season. I took different friends with me, although I would frequently go alone as well. I loved to sit on the bench along the walking trail overlooking the river and dream about moving there one day. It seemed impossible, though, as I was disabled and had to rely on my family for housing and money. When I was able to work, my jobs were closely tied to my connections and people in Staten Island.

It was not until my manic episode in my forties that I would attempt to live there. As I said previously, it was after I broke up with Lily and she left my apartment at my parents' house that I quit my jobs teaching music and moved to New Paltz. I rented a small studio apartment with a beautiful porch on Church Street right down the block from the main avenue and the bars and shops.

In my manic state, I was always talking to people, and I made a lot of friends. One of them was John, a young well-liked man who lived in my building. He had a small room, and he shared the bathroom with three other people. His room was a complete disaster, but it did not stop his beautiful girlfriend from the college from staying with him all the time.

The girls of New Paltz were very different. They were hippies and into art, music, and flower power. Money was not important to them. One day John and I were hanging out in front of our apartment house when a beautiful girl walked by and said hello. Her name was Tracy, and she was a good friend of John's. We talked for a bit and then she asked if she could crash on my couch that night, as she was visiting New Paltz for a while. I did not have a couch, but I was not going to let this opportunity pass me by.

Tracy was one of the most beautiful young women I had ever seen. She had long blonde hair and beautiful light eyes; she looked like something out of a renaissance painting. She was thin and wore those black leggings that I love on girls. Tracy had a degree in music and was an aspiring musician and vocal coach. She came upstairs with me, and we flopped on my bed and began to talk.

She showed me her music on her laptop, and she had a great voice. Her original music was old fashioned but beautiful and very well done. I played some of my songs on guitar for her, and she said that she loved them and that I should take vocal lessons with her to improve my voice. We were having such a wonderful time together, so I tried to kiss her while we laid on the bed. She just laughed and said, "Not yet, David."

In about an hour some other people came by, and a group of about five of us were hanging out in my apartment. I was having a great time with these cool people, and I was so happy that Tracy was spending the night. Everybody was talking, and we began to get hungry, so Tracy and a guy with a car went to the supermarket to buy food.

When they got back, Tracy took over the kitchen and cooked all of us a sumptuous feast of pasta and cheese and other good stuff. We all spent hours more hanging out, and it was a good time for everyone. Eventually the get-together broke up, and Tracy and I were left alone. We sat on my bed and talked for hours. She wept as she told me about her experience meeting a water nymph near a beautiful lake.

It was such a lovely story, especially because she looked like a water nymph herself and was such a beautiful soul. She told me she was polyamorous and had a main lover who she had some struggles with, but she loved him dearly. She was brilliant and told me something I never thought about—that monogamy was violence. I could see her point and understood that she was talking about the violence that jealousy could inspire.

After talking deep into the night, we cuddled together to sleep. Holding her in my arms was like something out of a dream. She was so beautiful, and I was so starved for love and the touch of a beautiful woman. She told me that I could hold her but that she would not have sex with me that night. That was fine with me, as I felt so much love toward this young woman that I was quite content to hold her in my arms and sleep with her all night.

Being manic, I did not sleep all that much, so I woke at dawn and watched this angel sleeping in my bed for a bit. Then I went down to the river for my daily prayer rituals. I picked flowers for her and returned to the apartment. I placed them in some water in a glass next to the bed, and she slowly woke up. "I brought you flowers," I said, and she looked very happy.

"Nobody gives me flowers!" she exclaimed. I laughed and thought she should probably be given flowers every day.

After a little small talk, she removed her shirt and told me I could kiss her breasts. I happily did and then we made out for a long time. It had been such a beautiful evening and morning that I forgot all about my troubles in Staten Island.

As we started to get dressed and greet the new day, John arrived. He had a cast on his foot because someone had knocked him off a balcony six weeks ago. He needed to get the cast off but had no health insurance or money. Tracy took matters into her own hands and got a very sharp serrated knife from my kitchen. She and John went to the bathroom to wet the cast and saw it off. John was fully dressed, but being the free spirit she was, Tracy got naked in the shower with him.

I watched this scene unfold—Tracy being so unbelievably gorgeous without clothes and John lying with his foot up in the shower with a silly grin on his face. Tracy sawed and sawed and somehow was able to get the cast off and free John's foot.

Life in New Paltz was great for a while. I would get up early and do my prayer rituals at the river and then go to Starbucks for a cup of coffee and hang out. I would bring my laptop with me and enjoy the morning listening to music and watching videos with my headphones on.

One day John and I decided to throw a party at my apartment. He knew a lot of people, so we invited a ton of folks. By evening my apartment was full of wonderful mostly college-age girls and guys. Everyone brought their own cases of beer, and we had a great time as I played Lady Gaga's albums on my Bose stereo.

It was a Thursday, which was always a big party night in this little college town. But I guess we were being really loud because the guy who lived downstairs climbed up the tree adjacent to my balcony and confronted me in the kitchen. He was really pissed off and said he had to work in the morning. I told him I would shut off the music, but he was still pissed and complained to the landlord the next day.

There were so many beautiful girls there that I did manage to get a couple of phone numbers. Nothing really came of that, though, but I made a lot of new friends.

There were many bars and cafés in town, and I did a lot of open mic nights with my guitar or keyboard. These were so much fun, and it was great to watch everybody else do their music or poetry or even some comedy acts. I did original songs, and it usually went over well. I was so happy living there for a while, and I thought it was like a dream come true.

New Paltz was known as the Jerusalem of Native Americans, and it was a really spiritual place. It was magical, and every day was a fun adventure. I spent a lot of time in the coffee shop that was just down the block from my apartment. I became friends with the barista there, and we talked all the time.

New Paltz was so different and wonderful. It was a community where everybody helped one another. I went to a bar called Snug's a lot and would have a beer or two and smoke cigarettes in the back, which was outdoors. It seemed there was always a party going on, and I would go dancing, which is something I would have never done if I was not manic. Having manic energy made me very social and talkative, and I made friends quickly.

Unfortunately, my money situation was not good. I tried and tried but could not find a job, and my small disability check was not enough to keep up with the rent and bills. Eventually I had to leave my apartment and live on the streets. I should not have taken the larger studio. I could have made it if I'd taken the open small room with the shared bathroom, but now it was too late.

I slept in the twenty-four-hour Laundromat behind Starbucks at night and hung out with my friends during the day at the various cafés and bars. Being homeless in New Paltz was not such the stigma that it was in the outside world. There were a lot of hippies who lived in their cars or stayed with friends or camped out in the woods.

In the good weather, I would sometimes stay at a place called the Sanctuary, a nature preserve on the outskirts of the town. It was so beautiful and peaceful that I liked to sleep there and watch the stars at night when I could get a blanket for coziness. The trees were gentle and lovely, and I swore they would whisper to me while I was sleeping.

One evening I was hanging out by the Main Street Market when a beautiful college girl walked toward the steps to the second-floor balcony, where there was an overlook and more restaurants. I walked next to her and said, "Hi. Where are you going?" She told me she was going to look at the stars. I felt an immediate connection to her and knew we were going to hook up. I asked if I could join her, and she agreed.

I can only describe this girl as a fairy. She was beautiful and petite with long hair and wore a ski hat with cute glasses. She had an incredibly perfect body and wore those leggings that I loved. We stood there for maybe a minute looking at the stars and then I kissed her gently on the lips. It was sweet and beautiful. We made out for a long time, and I reached my hands around to her ass under her leggings. She seemed to like this and started giggling. Eventually she said she had to go because she was meeting her friends. I said I wanted to make love somewhere, and she said she wanted to as well, but she had to meet her friends.

I picked her up and told her that I was not going to let her go because she was too cute. She laughed and laughed. I kept hugging her and hugging her and felt like I was falling in love. Eventually we said our goodbyes, and the magical moment was over. I did not even get her name much less her number, but I was happy to have shared a magical New Paltz moment with her.

New Paltz was filled with wonderful characters. There was the guy who grew and dried his own tobacco and who seemed to be around just about every corner. He did not sell the stuff, but anytime I asked him, he would roll me a homemade cigarette. His tobacco was so moist and sweet; it was like nothing I've ever smoked before or since.

Then there was the kind woman who owned the barbershop. She hung out with bikers, and their motorcycles were always parked in front of the shop. One day I saw her bending over in front of her business, walking her pet turtle. The turtle was very cute, and the whole thing made me think, *Only in New Paltz!*

Then there was the dude who came to all the open mic nights at the Cafeteria Coffee Shop. He was always dressed very well, and he sang opera every time. It was equally terrible each time, but he was absolutely adored by everyone in the town. He lived there as far as I could tell, but he was a young man and must have had some sort of disability. Unfortunately, he died young, and they put up a framed picture of him in the coffee shop.

One day I was hanging out by a restaurant with some apartments above it and talking to people, mostly college-age kids. I met a guy named George, who told me he was a guitar player, and we decided to jam. I still had my apartment then, so he came over and we played "The House of the Rising Sun." He played guitar, and I played my old cheap keyboard and sang. It was truly the best musical experience that I ever had jamming with someone, and we plotted to start a band one day.

George was dating the most beautiful girl in the town, but one night they had a fight, and she threw him out of the apartment. He asked if he could crash on my floor that night. We talked all night, and it was such an amazing discussion. We discussed philosophy and Greek mythology and God and Christ and everything under the sun. It was a great New Paltz night. Everybody who lived in this town seemed so bright and open-minded to new ideas.

Moving ahead a few years, when I returned from my horrible time in California, I decided to seek refuge at the strip bar in New Paltz. It was a very cool place for adult entertainment, and I had been there many times before as money would allow.

The girls who worked there were beautiful and kind, and the prices were very inexpensive if you wanted some alone time with them in the

VIP rooms. It was thirty dollars for twenty minutes, so if you had a few bucks, you could spend an hour with one of these angels.

Sometimes I just wanted to talk or hold them in my arms. Other times I was down for more adult action. When I returned from California, I wanted to celebrate getting out of jail and that hellhole. I showed up early, but the place wasn't open yet. Three of the strippers were in the parking lot waiting for the owner to show up with the key.

I did not know these strippers, but I would get to know them very soon. One petite girl with brown hair and eyes was so cute. She seemed cold, so I offered to give her my coat. She readily accepted, and somehow we ended up cuddling and then making out in the parking lot. Once the owner showed up and opened the door for all of us, I knew I was going to pick her for the VIP room first.

Once they got out of the dressing room, off we went into the room with the leather couch and dim lighting. I won't get too graphic here, as I am not writing a porn book, but we had amazing sex the whole time. I was with her in the VIP room three times that day, but the last time we just cuddled.

Then I was with an amazingly beautiful young woman twice more in the room, and the sex and kissing were just incredible. We did everything. She told me she was a natural blonde and gave me her phone number. The last time for the day, I was with another young goddess who I really can't even describe; she was so beautiful and sweet. We did not talk much, but talking was unnecessary.

These girls were so beautiful and sweet to me. I think that adult workers get a bad rap in this country. Men don't treat them well sometimes, and they are really doing a community service. They are more like adult social workers. There is a need for people to go to these places as men are often lonely or in bad marriages or situations. These wonderful girls provide such an important service and should really be given more respect. Remember, they are human beings too.

After my day of living like a rock star and rewarding myself, I met one more stripper on the way out. Her name was Arcadia, and we got to talking. She was a southern belle with a hot body and a cool thick accent. We exchanged numbers and I left for the evening.

Arcadia called a few days later and told me that she was at a bar drinking but that she was going back to her hotel room and I should meet her there. I was not sure exactly where her hotel was located, but I got in my car anyway. I spent about an hour going through different towns and stopping at the wrong hotels, but eventually I found her room.

She was lying in bed when I walked in, and the first thing she said to me was, "Well, come on now and whip it out." I thought this was really funny and said that I usually prefer some foreplay first. We went on to have what was probably the wildest and craziest night of sex I ever had. I did not have to pay for it, if you're wondering; she just liked me. After that we talked on the phone a few times. She wanted to make me dinner one night, but the craziness of my life did not allow it.

The last story I will share about New Paltz was when I was homeless there and living in the Laundromat. There was a bulletin board, and people would post all kinds of things on it. One day I noticed a long letter tacked to the board, so I read it. It was a suicide note from a girl who attended SUNY New Paltz. In it she described how horrible her life was and the abuse she faced at home and the boys who used her for her body at the school. I wept openly as I read it and wrote her a note back, hoping someone would bring it to her. I told her that she was not the only one who had been abused and that I would be her friend if she needed someone to talk to.

I don't know what happened exactly, but the next day the note was gone, and I guess she read my letter and changed her mind. That day there was a brand-new ten-speed bicycle at the Laundromat, and a cop told me it was a gift for me for helping to save that girl's life. I was overjoyed that she had not killed herself, but I had not ridden a bike since I was a kid, and it took me a while to adjust to it. It was a beautiful and sweet gift, but I wish I could have talked to her and been her friend too. Either way, I felt happy that this young girl had not given up hope after all.

Chapter 14

OLIVIA

(1994)

In the next four chapters, I will tell you about the most significant romantic relationships of my life. I deeply loved all of them in different ways.

It was 1994 and I was twenty-four years old. I had stopped taking my medication because I was stupid and did not realize I needed to stay on it for my entire lifetime. I was still not convinced, as a lot of people aren't, that I was truly sick and needed medication. After being off my meds for only few weeks, I started to become manic again.

After a month or so of erratic behavior and thoughts, I ended up in South Beach Psychiatric Center on Staten Island. I hated it there with a passion and thought they were drugging me unnecessarily. At first, I would not take the medication, but after realizing that I would never get out if didn't, I reluctantly took the pills.

One day we were being escorted to the lunchroom when a staff member opened one of the locked steel doors with their big key. Immediately a patient ran through the door and tried to escape. All the staff went after him, and the patients were left standing in the hallway.

I saw this as my chance to escape as well, and while they chased after the other patient, I quietly and quickly made my way out the door. I ran as fast as I could through the maze of buildings and trees and through a field of weeds. Eventually I came to a twenty-foot-high fence that I climbed easily. I was free.

I walked a few blocks through the Staten Island suburban neighborhood and came to a phone booth. I had some change on me and called a cab to take me to a female friend's house a few miles away. When we arrived, I rang the bell and asked if she could pay for the cab, which she did.

I called my friend Robert, and he brought me to his small house in the Great Kills part of the island. The house was tiny, and we playfully called it the shack. Robert let me stay there, and although he did not have much money, he bought me food and let me wear his clothes, as I had nothing but the clothes on my back.

Robert was a musician as well, and he played guitar and drums and was a very cool guy. He worked as a chef, but I don't think he made much at that. Robert eventually gave me a few dollars he could spare and some clothes and drove me over the bridge into New Jersey, where there was not a warrant out for me leaving a state hospital.

I took the train to Princeton, a town I knew a little bit, and figured I could survive on the campus and maybe get help from the college kids. The first night I slept in a church graveyard, which made me feel safe and protected. I had no money, and by the next day, I was starving.

One nice man in a shop gave me a free bagel. I was searching through the dumpsters on campus when I came across an incredible find—an almost whole Domino's pizza still in the box. I was never so happy in my life to eat pizza. If you know what it's like to be hungry and to have no food, money, or shelter, you may understand the joy and intense gratitude I felt to God for finding this treasure.

That evening, I hung out on the campus and talked to some interesting students. They were very friendly, and we had some great conversations about math and physics. They even put my name down to get into a private party where there was free food and drink. This helped me out so much.

The next day was Sunday, and I thought my best bet for survival was to go to the churches and try to get food or money. The churches I went to were very generous and gave me some money to buy food. Thank God there are good people in this world. One priest advised me to go to a Catholic Charities place in Philadelphia where they might let me stay or help me with food.

The next day I took the train to Philadelphia and found the address for the Catholic Charities. They took me in, and I was able to stay there and shower and eat and talk to some of the other people they were helping. During the day I walked around the city and enjoyed my freedom. I was manic, though, so I had lots of energy and was much more friendly and talkative than my usual personality.

I was sitting on the steps of the University of the Arts when I saw a woman walking slowly by who would change my life forever. She was just under five feet tall with long red hair and big hazel eyes. She was easily the most beautiful girl I had ever seen in person, on TV, in the movies, or in any setting whatsoever. She wore a hippie flowered dress but walked very slowly and shuffled her feet while she used two canes for balance.

I was immediately struck by cupid's arrow and fell madly in love with her at once. I was completely taken by this vision of beauty from the moment my eyes caught sight of that perfect face. I said out loud to nobody, "Okay, David. Go chase another angel with a broken wing."

I approached her and asked if there were any pianos around the school and if I could play them. She gave me an angelic smile, and I saw in her eyes and on her porcelain white face such a pure soul that I knew my first instincts were correct. We got to talking, and she told me she was a freshman at the university. She had a sweet, soft, and melodious voice, like the songs of the sirens. She did not give me her number when I asked, but she took my number at the Catholic Charities where I was staying and promised she would call me.

Olivia called the next day, and we talked for a bit and made plans to meet at the Liberty Bell the next day. The next day I was at a mall when I got to talking to a man to whom I told my situation. He bought me lunch, as I had no money, and I was very appreciative.

We continued to talk, and I told him about my date that day with the beautiful Olivia. He told me he was the prophet Daniel reborn and gave me forty dollars to take her out. I was so happy that I had some money, but I first spent it on some small costume jewelry to give to her as a gift.

We met at the Liberty Bell and walked around the city. She was so sweet and wonderful, and everything she said reminded me of a song. We spent a lot of time singing and laughing. Eventually we came to a McDonald's and had some lunch. Olivia was a vegetarian, so I think all she had were some French fries and a Coke. Afterward, we went on the little rides they had in front of the place, and we had a great time.

We went back to her college and found a piano, and I played for a long time and sang her some of my songs. We had a great time, but I told her the people at the charities had discovered I was an escaped person from a mental hospital, so they could not let me stay anymore. Unbelievably, even after hearing this, Olivia invited me to stay at her dorm room.

She shared a suite with two other girls, and she said we could stay in the living room on the floor so as not to disturb her roommates in the bedroom. We camped out on the floor with blankets and pillows and had the most wonderful time talking and laughing all night.

Eventually we kissed, and it was absolutely magical. Her soft lips touched mine in a way that was so sweet and gentle that I knew our love was real. We did not have sex but just cuddled and kissed all night. She told me some horrible stories about her life and how she had been raped over and over again by a man who lived in the homeless shelter where she and her mom worked. Her mother was a social worker.

I felt so horrible for her. She was eighteen now, and this man had traumatized her so badly that she was afraid of sex and men. The fact that she trusted me enough to sleep with her told me that she had fallen in love with me at first sight just as I had with her. We stayed there two days and nights until her roommates, who she hated, finally told her I had to go.

I had nowhere to stay and said I'd try to get to Buffalo where I had some connections and maybe could get a job. She insisted on coming with me, and we went to the ATM. She withdrew all the money she had and put it in my hands. She was trusting me to take care of her, so off we went on the buses to get to Buffalo.

As I mentioned earlier, Olivia was disabled. She could not walk without her two metal canes, and she had deep scars up and down both legs from surgery to correct her condition, which kept her out of a wheelchair. She could barely walk without the canes, but she did not let it stop her at all.

We had so much fun on the buses, talking, laughing, holding hands, and singing songs. We had the best time ever. We stopped in Boston and went to a motel for the night, but the old woman behind the counter did not want us to stay there because we were not married. We thought this was really weird for 1994, but eventually I argued our way into getting the room.

Sleeping with Olivia was such heaven. I was in love with her like I had never been with anyone else before in my life. We kissed and held each other all night, and it was absolutely perfect. We were two lost souls who had found each other by the grace of God. Our time together was so healing for both of us, as we had been through so much trauma in our lives.

After a few days of traveling, we finally arrived in Buffalo. We went to the piano room near the music department and hung out there for a long time and even slept in the room.

The next morning two cops arrested me for trespassing. Olivia was crying, having become overwhelmed by being homeless, and asked the cops to try to contact her aunt who lived in Buffalo. I was really upset, but what was done was done.

The cops brought me to a jail for a few hours, but they told everybody that I was a great guy, as Olivia had said. She'd told them I was a perfect gentleman and to please be kind to me. The police were very nice and immediately transferred me to a mental hospital in Buffalo. They had found the warrant indicating that I had escaped from South Beach.

South Beach sent a guy to pick me up on a plane, and he met me at the hospital. We drove to the airport, and it would have been quite easy for me to escape again, but I thought I would just go back to Staten Island and face the music.

Once at the hospital, I was treated to a hero's welcome by the other patients and some of the staff. They told me no other escaped patient had ever made it that far before. They also told me they had spoken to Olivia's mother and that I was not to contact her. This broke my heart because I was so in love with her.

To my surprise, Olivia called me on the pay phone in the hospital a few days later. She had tracked me down and wanted to apologize for freaking out and getting me sent back from Buffalo. I was not mad at her at all, as I understood how hard it can be to survive on the streets, even if you have a traveling partner.

She asked if she could visit, as she was now back at the University of the Arts in Philadelphia. We arranged for her to stay with my parents on the weekend, and they would bring her twice a day for visiting hours. My parents were so nice to do this for us. They picked her up at the train in New Jersey, and she slept in my bed for the weekend while I was still locked up in the hospital.

When she came to visit, I don't think I was ever as happy in my life. She told me she loved me, and I loved her too. She had gone so far out of her way to keep our relationship going, and I felt nothing but joy. I had to stay in the psych ward for another six weeks, but Olivia visited every weekend, mailed beautiful letters during the week, and spoke to me on the phone every day.

Her letters were filled with cute colorful drawings of flowers and birds and other pretty things. I sent her back letters and poetry that went on and on for pages. I never felt so inspired to write in my life. She would sit on my lap sometimes during the visits, and we would sneak kisses.

The day finally came when I was stable enough to leave the hospital. I wanted to go home, but my parents said no. They were not ready to take me back and feared I would stop taking my medication again.

This was when my friend Robert really came through for me again and let me stay with him as long as I wanted. This was big because if I did not have a legitimate place to go, I could have been warehoused at the hospital for many, many months until they got me state housing. I returned to the shack and was so happy to be free and mostly sane again. Robert had a piano I could play, and Olivia stayed over on the weekends at Robert's small house.

My parents continued to pick her up at the train in New Jersey, and we spent so many happy nights sleeping on the foldout couch in Robert's living room. A short time later, my grandma died of lung cancer, and I stayed with my mom for a few days to go to the funeral and the shiva. While I was away, one of Robert's friends was at his house when a criminal broke in, held him at knifepoint, and stole the television, stereo, and anything else of value.

This really scared me, and my parents had mercy on me and let me move back into their house and my old room. Now Olivia and I could really spend time together. My parents allowed me to use their car, and we went to the beach and sometimes out to eat.

We started to have a real sex life, although we never made it past third base. Olivia had never been with a man unless you counted the rape, which I didn't. She still was very traumatized and sometimes had flashbacks while we were fooling around. After my grandmother died, Olivia and I stayed at her apartment in Brooklyn for a while, and we got to spend so many beautiful days and nights together. She was the love of my life and my first real girlfriend.

Olivia was more than just beautiful. She was funny and brilliant and sweet and fun. We talked about so many things, from music to philosophy to religion to politics. She was really a magical creature, like a fairy.

Eventually my family had to move everything out of my grandma's apartment, and I came back home to live. Olivia visited every weekend for a long time, and we always had great fun. We would sing together all the time, and I was so happy that God had finally answered my lifelong prayers for true love. I may have had to wait a long time for her to come, but it was worth it.

After about two years of dating, Olivia's mother wanted her far away from me, as she did not approve of the relationship, even though she had never met me. She enrolled Olivia at New England College, which was a great distance from Philadelphia and Staten Island.

Olivia was unhappy living in Philadelphia and wanted to be in a more natural setting. Henniker, New Hampshire, was in the middle of nowhere, so I knew her mom would get her wish. It was also a more suitable place for Olivia.

The last time Olivia visited me in Staten Island, we were in my backyard when she told me she was breaking up with me. I was devastated and asked her why. She said she did not love me like she used to. She told me I would find someone else, but I knew I could never find anyone as special as her.

We stayed friends and talked on the phone when she was at her new college. It wasn't long before she had a new boyfriend and a new girlfriend. I knew Olivia was bisexual and polyamorous, so it was no surprise that she'd found people to love right away.

I visited her twice while she was there and once flied on a tiny plane to New Hampshire and then took a cab into the woods to her school. We had a fun time. She was working a lot, so I spent a good amount of my time there practicing the guitar I had started learning how to play and waiting for her.

The last time I visited her, I drove up in my old little car through some horrible storms, and it took me twelve hours. Unfortunately, we had an argument and did not get along that well. I came home and we never spoke again.

Olivia's effect on my life cannot be overstated. I was twenty-four when I met her, and she was eighteen. All my life I had wanted true love, and for the first time, I actually had it. She loved me with all her heart, and I loved her with all of mine. She was and is an amazing, magical person, and I could not have found anyone better for a first girlfriend and first true love. I will remember her forever.

Chapter 15

ERIN

(1995-1998)

I was in a daze for a while after Olivia broke up with me. I thought I would never again meet somebody so special or who would love me like that. I was taking my medicine, but I was still depressed and anxious. I hung around the house feeling sorry for myself.

One of my mom's friends suggested I go to her doctor. He was a world-famous psychiatrist who did not take my insurance and cost $185 per appointment. He had written many best-selling books on manic depression and was the one who'd introduced the use of lithium in bipolar patients.

Dr. O'Conner had an office on Park Avenue in Manhattan and worked out of New York-Presbyterian Hospital. The first consultation was $500, and my parents were willing to pay for it because they loved me so much and wanted me to get better.

Dr. O'Connor was a well-dressed, distinguished-looking man in his sixties, and my first appointment with him lasted over an hour. He changed my medications immediately. The most important adjustment he made was to put me on Prozac, an antidepressant. The state doctors I had been seeing would not put me on an antidepressant because they were afraid, I'd have a manic episode.

Dr. O'Connor thought it was worth the risk, and I started taking the new prescriptions. Within about six weeks, everything started to change in my brain. I began feeling like me again. I was no longer depressed or chronically anxious, and I returned to a normal level of energy. The difference was unbelievably profound. I had hopes and dreams again. I wanted to pursue life again and not just rot on the couch.

I was me again after more than six years of hell cycling between mania and depression and going through the trauma of this mental illness. After jail, drug abuse and homelessness, long stays in psychiatric hospitals, a suicide attempt, and extended periods of clinical depression, I finally felt normal.

The first thing I decided to do was to go back to college. I enrolled at the College of Staten Island at the City University of New York, and although I did not know what I would major in, I was starved for learning and wanted to get my degree. Eventually I took a sociology class and fell in love with the discipline. I had some of the happiest moments of my life sitting in those lecture halls and listening to those wonderful professors. I had always loved books and learning, and now I felt such peace in my brain doing it at the college level.

I have always been a night person, so I took all my classes after twelve noon and did not have the problems I'd had in high school with being too tired to get up early. I hated to get up early. I took a class in parapsychology and found new friends. I met a lot of wonderful people, and it became one of the happiest times of my life.

One night I decided to go to temple with my family in New Jersey for Tisha B'Av, a day of remembrance for the destruction of King

Solomon's temple in Jerusalem. I don't know why I went that night, as I never liked going to shul, but I guess I just wanted to hang out with family.

We sat at a table with other temple goers. I noticed a beautiful girl with glasses and tried not to stare at her. She was a special guest of the temple and was there to sing. When I heard her voice, I thought it was an angel singing. Her voice was so beautiful and peaceful that it filled my heart with joy.

After the service I knew I wanted to talk to her, but I was too nervous to say hello. No longer manic, I was back to my shy self. Somehow, I worked up the courage and approached her as she stood with her family. "You have a beautiful voice," I said. She thanked me and smiled. We got into a long conversation, and I got up the nerve to ask for her phone number, which she gave me right away.

That was how I met Erin. I was going to call her the next day, but I was so nervous that my stomach was in knots, and I had butterflies. I was so afraid that I would not know what to say to her that I wrote a list of subjects on a piece of paper to talk about in case I froze up.

I finally dialed her number, and she seemed happy to hear from me. We conversed for hours. I didn't need the list at all, as Erin could really talk, and she was so smart and full of information.

Erin lived in New Jersey. My parents had bought a new car for themselves and given me their old one, so I went to Colonia, New Jersey, to pick her up for our first date. I was very nervous meeting her parents before we went out. Erin was about twenty-three, and I was a few years older. Her father was kind of a strange-looking man, almost like a typical nerd with a pocket protector. He was an accountant, and although he was polite, I would soon learn that he did not like me because I had long hair and was from New York.

Her mom was very sweet and seemed genuine, and I was comfortable in her presence. Erin looked beautiful. She had long wavy light-brown hair and lovely brown eyes and a very cute body. She was very pretty and my type. We went out for dinner and had a wonderful time. Erin was brilliant and funny and fun to be with, and we hit it off right away. She had graduated from Rider University and worked for a time for Johnson and Johnson, but she hated corporate America and now made a living by tutoring Hebrew, math, and Spanish. She worked very hard to make a living and was a sweet and caring person.

The next few months were very good. We went out every weekend and got to know each other. She would not let me kiss her until the third date, so by then it was very sweet and special. Erin had a small apartment in Lawrenceville, New Jersey, about an hour's drive from my house, and would stay there during the week and go home for the weekends to be with her parents and to see me.

Eventually I started sleeping over at her apartment when I could, and we got even closer. Erin was a virgin, although she'd had a boyfriend before me. She was not exactly waiting for marriage, but she had sexual problems. Even though I slept over many times, we never went further than second base during the whole relationship. "I just don't get horny like other girls," she told me.

We would cuddle all the time and give each other back rubs and kiss, and for the time being, I was okay with this because I was beginning to fall in love with her and was happy to just hold her through the night.

My mother was not a big fan of Erin for a few reasons, one being that she almost always dressed in sweatpants, which did not bother me at all. Another was that she was controlling. She would not drive to Staten Island because she was too nervous on the highway, and she had a general fear of New York that she'd inherited from her father. When I arrived at her apartment, she always made me take a shower and brush my teeth because I smelled liked cigarettes, which she hated.

Erin was superintelligent but very eccentric. She loved teddy bears and had hundreds in her apartment. She wanted to take one out with us for dinner and sit it at the table, but I wouldn't let her because it would be too embarrassing. She even talked about having a table for the teddy bears at our wedding, which I thought was preposterous. I was not thinking about getting married anytime soon anyway.

Going out to dinner with her was something of an adventure as well, as she was very determined that I be an old-fashioned gentleman. She would stand by the door and wait for me to open it, no matter what. After a pleasant dinner, she would check the chairs and under the table to see if she had forgotten anything. Then she would steal a bunch of sugar packets and napkins and stick them in her purse to bring home. She claimed she was poor and needed those things and that she had no safety net like I did living at home, even though I'm sure her parents would not have let her starve.

Erin had very bad periods and would suffer greatly from pain and exhaustion once a month. Her mood would suffer too, and we would have huge arguments every time she went through this because she could be unreasonable. It got so bad that at one point we thought about not talking during her period every month, but I decided against this as I loved to be with her and talk to her.

Looking back, she probably had some big hormone problem that also led to a lack of libido, but at the time she did not get tested.

While I was dating Erin, I was still working very hard on my degree, and I was reasonably happy, although I still had some psychiatric symptoms and side effects from the medications for my disability. Every spring I would get slightly manic despite the meds and experience very disturbing tactile hallucinations. For me, these manifested as vividly feeling objects in my head, mostly knives or stones or anything hard. I could feel it in my mind, and it was physically painful, like it was real.

Dr. O'Connor would raise the medication at this time to combat the symptoms, which helped a lot, but there were side effects related to this increase, such as difficulty achieving an orgasm. As you might imagine, this could be very frustrating for a young man.

Erin and I continued to be happy and were in love for sure. I treasured her kindness and her sweetness and her sense of humor and her physical beauty. We mostly had good times, and she enjoyed when I sang to her over the phone during the week. I loved her voice as well and would have her sing to me all the time.

Erin came with me on many family outings, and everyone liked her a lot—everyone except my mom, although I don't think she was ever rude to her or made her feel bad. Mom just complained about her to me afterward. We used to play ping-pong sometimes, and she was very competitive. She was a good player and we had great matches.

Although we were happy together, I longed for something more. I loved her but knew I needed a more compatible sexual partner. I went on a few dates and hooked up with girls at the college. I'm not proud that I cheated on her, but I had needs that were not being met. My mother was very pissed at me when I brought a girl home to my bedroom. She didn't know about the lack of sex life that Erin and I had.

One great thing about Erin was that she accepted my disability and my reliance on medication for stability and sanity. This made me feel very safe and comforted, as it was difficult to explain to prospective girlfriends about my disability and why I was in school at a later age than was usual. Erin was not materialistic at all, and she had good values and morals. She was a sweetheart.

It was around this time when I had my first episode of rapid atrial fibrillation. I was sitting in class one day when I felt my heart jumping around in my chest. It was fluttering, and I felt a weird sensation. I went to the college nurse, who listened to my heart and said I should go to the emergency room because she thought I had an irregular heartbeat.

I did not want to go to the ER, so I went to my regular doctor instead. He was not in, so I saw another physician in the practice, who said I had rapid atrial fibrillation, and my heart rate was over 250. I asked her what they would do about it at the hospital, and she replied that they might have to put a needle in my heart. This freaked me out to no end.

My parents brought me to the emergency room, where they hooked me up to all kinds of machines and tubes. I was really scared and thought they were going to stick a needle in my chest. They did say they might have to give me an electric shock from the paddles, and this freaked me out even more. By some miracle they were able to stop it by pressing and holding my carotid artery down. They tried that again and again until it finally worked and my heart beat

normally. The doctor said it was the first time he had ever seen that work.

It happened again about a month later. I was extremely nervous and went straight to the hospital. This time the carotid thing did not work, and I had to stay for a few days while they tried different things. The whole time the electric paddles were right next to me, and I was so freaked out that they might have to use them. They eventually gave me an extremely painful shot into my right forearm that brought my heart rate back to a sinus rhythm.

These episodes made me a nervous wreck, and I was constantly checking my pulse and praying it would not happen again. I saw a specialist in Manhattan, who put me on medication and told me if it continued, I would need an ablation, where they would run a wire up my groin and into my heart to burn out the circuits that were causing the irregular heartbeat. This also added to my fear and paranoia. I was already a nervous person, and now I really had something to worry about.

Erin was comforting during this time but did not come to visit me in the hospital due to her own fears of driving in New York. This did not make me happy at all. It was about this time when I met Susan in my sociology of marriage and family class. I broke up with Erin over the phone, and she was extremely upset because I ended our relationship so impersonally, and she also suspected I had met someone else, which I had.

We stayed in touch via phone for many years after, and she was always strange and mysterious. She would never tell me where she was, just that she had a new boyfriend. For many years she called me about once a month from a private number and would not tell me how to reach her.

She was always very secretive, but now it was really bad. I accepted it and took her monthly late-night calls for years until I become engaged more than ten years later. After she knew I was getting married, she never called again. I do think she was holding out hope that we would get back together and get married. Erin was a beautiful, brilliant, talented woman, but it was not in the cards for us. I did love her, though, and perhaps if we'd had a normal sex life, it could have worked out.

Chapter 16

SUSAN

(1997-2009)

As I mentioned in the last chapter, I met Susan while I was still dating Erin. She was in my sociology class, and what I noticed about her first was not her looks but her voice. She had an innocent way of speaking, and the things she said let me know she had a heart of gold. She also had a sweet lilting voice that was very different from other girls.

I would say hello to her during class, and she would always smile back and say hi. One day after class, I was sitting on the bench in front of the building smoking a cigarette when Susan approached me and said hello. We started to chat, and I invited her to sit down next to me.

We talked about different things. I told her I might want to be a professor someday, which I did if I continued in grad school for sociology. We spoke for a long time, and she was really adorable. She had long dark curly hair and puppy dog brown eyes. She suggested we exchange numbers, and I called her the next day. We made a date to go to the Cargo Café, a popular spot on Bay Street in Staten Island. I used to hang out there with my friends all the time. I picked her up at her house. Her parents and sister were there to greet me and were all smiles. They were very nice and happy to see me.

At the Cargo, Susan had a drink or two and I had a Sprite, as I was driving and did not drink anymore anyway. We had a really good time and talked a lot. I learned that her father was a chef and that she was very close to her family. They were Italian and she loved Italian food, as I did.

After the date I took her home and walked her to the door. I hugged her and promised to call soon. I called her the next day, and we were excited to go out again.

For our next date, we decided to hang out at my house and listen to music. We talked a lot, and I discovered she loved heavy metal bands, which was surprising given her sweet and wholesome personality and aura. I told her about Erin, and she said she would not kiss me until I broke up with her. I said that I planned to but that I needed a few days. A little later while we were hanging out in my bedroom, I guess she decided she could not wait. She literally jumped me, and we started making out on the bed.

I was twenty-seven, and Susan was twenty-two and a virgin. After I broke up with Erin, we started dating regularly. We went out to dinner a lot and liked to cuddle and make out in my bed. I was not so ready to get into a relationship again, but she kept pressuring me, especially because she was bringing me to a big family barbecue and wanted to introduce me to her cousins as her boyfriend. I eventually agreed.

Susan was a wounded soul, but no one really knew that because she always had a smile on her face and was so sweet. She had been molested as a child, and it had left a deep scar on her soul. She was very afraid of men, and it seemed I was the only one she could trust. At the barbecue, her cousin said he bet that Susan had never even had a bad dream because she was so happy all the time, but I knew better. She was a very anxious and tormented person. I think that's why she liked heavy metal music because it gave her a chance to get out her rage.

We were happily in a relationship now, and Susan was exactly the person I had guessed she was before I got to know her. She had a heart of gold. After we'd been going out for three months, she decided that she wanted to lose her virginity and that we should go all the way. We were in my bedroom, and I had candles going. We had an amazing time, and everything went smoothly.

After we made love for the first time, she stood up, and her long hair, which was probably full of chemicals, touched a candle and went up in flames. Luckily, I was standing directly behind her and was able to put out the fire with my hands. The room smelled a bit like burned hair, but I had gotten it out quickly enough that she did not really lose any hair. I did not burn my hands either.

Being Italian Catholic, Susan said maybe that was a sign from God that she should not have had premarital sex. I think she was mostly kidding, though. After that Susan and I became regular lovers, and the sex was amazing. She was wonderful in bed, and I finally was in a truly satisfying relationship.

I grew very close to Susan's family. Her dad was a retired chef and had owned a deli in Brooklyn. He was also an avid gardener and grew everything from tomatoes to zucchini to basil to chamomile. Most importantly he had many fig trees from Italy.

I had never tried figs before, but after that first fall, I was addicted to them. We ate them directly off the trees, and I had never tasted a fruit so delicious. Her dad taught me a lot about cooking and gardening, and we had long conversations in the kitchen while he cooked or in the garden where he would teach me about plants.

Susan's mother was a sweet woman who had to retire early as a teacher in a Catholic high school because she had heart trouble. Her cholesterol level was over five hundred, and she needed multiple stents to keep her from having a heart attack.

Susan's dad did all the cooking, so her mom was free to do other things. Unfortunately, she was frequently in pain and suffered from her heart condition. She and I used to have long conversations as well. I really loved her parents.

At family outings I ate amazing home-cooked Italian food and got to know her family well. Her sister and brother were cool people too and extremely intelligent. They accepted me into the family, even though I was Jewish and never made me feel uncomfortable.

We had a good relationship, but something was always missing for me. To say that Susan absolutely worshiped me would be an understatement. She called me her savior and was obviously head over heels in love. Although I certainly loved her, I was not as in love her with her as I had been with Olivia or even Erin. In addition, the difference in our intelligence made things difficult for me.

Susan was in college, but she was there primarily to gain credits for her job as a teacher's aide. When we first started going out, she was working as a nanny, but she eventually got a position working with special education children in the New York City school system. She was great at this because she loved children so much and was so kindhearted and nurturing. While we were together, I wrote all her college papers for her so that she could pass her classes.

Our dating life was kind of mellow. We would usually go out to dinner or hang out at my house or hers and watch TV. Susan was easy to please, and she knew I was not that into the club scene or bars or anything too exciting by then. We were very similar in that respect; she even called herself a house mouse. I was that way too and still am. I mostly prefer to hang out at home.

We did like to attend the performances at the Staten Island library. We saw a lot of classical guitar and lute music and some flamenco. We were definitely on the same wavelength as far as our social lives. We went to a Jewel concert once as well as a Crosby, Stills, and Nash performance in New Jersey.

We shared a love of music, and she enjoyed it when I played piano and sang to her our favorite songs. She loved to lay on the couch and listen and sometimes took naps while I played because it relaxed her.

We had a great relationship, and my family loved her, especially my parents, but to me something was missing. Because of our intellectual inequality, I became bored. I was tired of the same conversations and not having anything to talk about with her besides her family and some simple stuff. I was an avid reader and loved everything about the universe. I wanted to learn and discuss everything. My mind ached for intellectual stimulation, and I just was not getting it from her.

I broke up with her after two and a half years of dating, and she was really devastated. I had no choice, though. I knew I needed more out of life. We stayed friends and talked often. Over the next few years, we still hung out and had sex whenever we felt like it. That part of our relationship was never a problem, so it continued.

I started to look for other girls to date. I was still kind of shy and did not ask anyone out at the college, so I turned to internet dating, which was very new at the time. Mostly I had crappy dates, and it was very frustrating to try to find someone new.

After a string of bad dates and disappointing connections, I found a girl named Rebecca on Green Singles. This site was for spiritual and environmentally conscious people. We wrote a few emails back and forth and seemed to have a lot in common. This was in the 1990s, before the ability to send pictures over the internet, so she sent me one in the mail. In it she wore a black velvet dress and was absolutely stunning, with long curly dark hair and piercing green eyes. She had the body of a goddess and was also Jewish and from Long Island. We started talking on the phone and set up a first date near her home in Long Island.

I drove out to her and let her pick the restaurant. Rebecca was from a rich family, and her father was a multimillionaire who owned and managed many apartment buildings and other real estate. So of course she chose the most expensive restaurant in town.

I nearly had a heart attack when I saw the prices, and I was so pissed that she did this to me on a first date. I was going to college and living at home and collecting a small SSI disability check, so this restaurant was completely out of my budget. I told her I could not afford it. I think we both had soup and left.

Rebecca was a very difficult person to get along with. She had borderline personality disorder and was combative and argumentative. Honestly, she was a big pain in the ass, and the date ended rather abruptly when I dropped her back at her apartment. I decided to call her when I got home, and we had a real discussion then. We both admitted our mental illness to each other and shared how rough our lives had been. She had graduated from the University of Pennsylvania but had not worked in years. She was extremely intelligent but very bossy and obnoxious.

However, we did bond over that long conversation. She was on disability as well, and her father paid for her apartment and supported her. We had much in common, and I invited her over for the next weekend. We ended up fooling around, and I have to say her body was addictive to me. It became a love-hate relationship that was heavily sexually charged.

She wanted to be my girlfriend, but I knew it would never work because of her personality. We did become lovers, though, in a sort of friends with benefits relationship. Many of our conversations ended in phone sex, and we would visit each other and hang out and sleep together from time to time. Even though we were friends, she had a sexual hold on me for years and years, and whenever I was single, we would hook up again.

Rebecca would play a role in my life for the next twenty-five years on and off, depending on whether if she had a boyfriend or I had girlfriend. We were always there to hook up if we were free. She had a boyfriend for a long time, and we would still chat but then she would disappear for months or years, only to call me again and entice me with sex.

During this period, I concentrated a lot on school and earned really good grades, even making the dean's list. I loved school so much, and this was one of the happiest times of my life.

I was at a family party at my cousin's house in Staten Island when my younger cousin introduced me to her friend Wynona. She was a musician as well, so we had a lot to talk about. She gave me her number, and soon we started hanging out. I was very interested in her romantically, as she was brilliant and talented and cute, but she saw me only as a friend. She said, "You're attractive, but I'm not attracted to you."

We had a great friendship, though, and I really enjoyed her company. She was very talented but could also be very critical. She was Jewish but was a Jew for Jesus and was very serious about Christianity. Even so, when she had a boyfriend, she engaged in premarital sex. She also smoked pot constantly and had anxiety issues. We had a lot of fun but also many, many arguments, especially about religion. I sometimes would flat out call her stupid and would argue with her about the contradictions in the Bible.

Her family was cool, and I became close to her parents and her sister, even attending her sister's wedding. Wynona was a music major at my school and an amazing singer. Sometimes we would play together, but she could be so critical and obnoxious. I still loved her, though, and wanted her as my girlfriend, but the answer was always no. I was still doing the internet dating thing, but I could never find anyone I clicked with. Susan and I were still great friends and hooked up on occasion, so I decided we might as well try again and get back together.

I was very comfortable with her, and my family was overjoyed that we were a couple again. Her family accepted me back, and we continued to be close. I missed her parents especially, as I really cared about them and enjoyed their company.

A year passed and we were doing all right, but those same lingering questions I'd had about our relationship still existed, and it wasn't long before I developed a wandering eye, always on the lookout for her replacement. I was not seeing Rebecca, but our phone conversations frequently were sexual in nature.

I started a job at the college as an English tutor in the summer immersion program. This was a class for incoming students who did not do well on the English assessment test. I met Maria on the first day of class. She was a beautiful Puerto Rican woman who was a few years older than me and was returning to school after working on Wall Street. I won't go into details here because I will talk exclusively about that relationship in the next chapter. I told Maria I could only be in an open relationship, so I continued to see Susan as well.

When I told Susan that I wanted to see other people, she took it surprisingly well because she was just happy I was still with her. Eventually I told her about Maria, but I tried not to talk about it too much out of respect for Susan's feelings. That fall was my final year of school, and I was very happy to be getting my degree soon. After everything I had been through, I felt it was a remarkable accomplishment to be able to go through four years of college without a mental breakdown. Giving up drugs and alcohol was also a big bonus.

The year was not without its troubles, though. I had another instance of rapid atrial fibrillation that put me in the hospital for four days and brought about a lot of scary times for me. As before, they were able to get my heart rate back to normal with intravenous medicine over a few days, but it again made me a nervous wreck. At least they never had to shock me with the paddles.

At the end of that year, I found a lesion on my thumb that looked suspicious. I went to the dermatologist, who said that it could be cancer and if it was that they would have to remove my thumb. This was possibly the worst thing a doctor had ever said to me. Music was everything to me. To lose my thumb when I had been a piano player all my life and now was training in classical guitar was so frightening to me that I could not stand it.

The surgeon was a nice woman, and she took off the lesion using a local anesthetic. She said it was not that deep, but they had to send it to the lab to make sure it was not cancer. It was about a month from finals, and I was in full freak-out mode. I could not sleep. I could not study. I did not practice the guitar. All I did was worry. I was a nervous wreck and could not get it out of my mind. The results were supposed to be back in a week, but the doctor said they were inconclusive, and it would take more time.

I could not believe this was happening. I am a very nervous person and the fact that I did not go back to drugs and alcohol during this time was a miracle. After two weeks of waiting, I got the call that it was not cancer but an age spot. I was so relieved that my life was not going to change, but I was pissed that they put me through that.

On top of that, I was still worried about my heart problems. I must have taken my pulse a hundred times a day. I managed to pull it together for finals week and did really well in all my classes. I graduated with a cumulative 3.43 GPA, including almost a perfect 4.0 in my major, and got my diploma.

I totally blew off graduation because I hate ceremonies and getting up early, but that beautiful diploma meant the world to me and still does.

Susan and I continued to date, and I was happier knowing I was free to go out with other people and not be tied down. I did not know what I wanted to do after graduation and considered living on a commune for a while. The fact that I could not bring my cat made that a bad plan for me.

I was still living in the downstairs apartment and deciding what to do with my life now that I was a college graduate at twenty-nine. I hated the city, so I knew I could never work there. I also knew my job offers would be limited because of the way they screwed me in Florida and made me a felon. My degree was worth nothing when it came to good jobs because of that conviction. However, I did not go to school for a job or to make money. I did it for the education and to satisfy my lifelong love of learning.

I decided to take a year and write a book about spirituality and society. I worked on it almost every day and eventually completed a 250-page volume. I didn't know what to do with it, as it's very hard to find an agent or a publisher, and I did not think it was that great. I did have an excerpt from it printed on a spiritual website, so I thought that was cool.

Susan and I continued to date, and I was seeing other girls as well, but after another year of this, I still did not feel content within the relationship and broke up with her again. She was very sad and so was I, but we continued to be friends with benefits on occasion. Another couple of years passed, and in the wake of the September 11 attacks on the World Trade Center, I entered the worst depression of my life. As a mentally ill person, I am extremely vulnerable to stressful events, and this as well as a car accident I had in August led me to become mentally ill again.

I will cover this more in a later chapter, but Susan's help during this time was profound. I was suicidal for months and months, and Susan would come over when she could and just hold me in my bed so that I would not kill myself. After about a year, I started to recover and had gained a new appreciation for her.

It was always Susan's heart that was the most attractive thing about her. She was infinitely kind, which I find to be so appealing in a woman. So, for the third time, we got back together. We went out for years and then I asked her to move in with me. She told me she couldn't because her parents were old fashioned and would never allow it. I was tired of living alone, and I really thought I would never find anybody as sweet and kind and who loved me as much, so we talked about marriage. I felt I owed it to her in a lot of ways, and although she was not the ideal person for me, I was getting older and thought that settling down was a good idea.

My mother and father helped me buy a beautiful ring for her, and I proposed in Red Bank, New Jersey, one of our favorite places to go. At this time, I was working as a guitar and piano teacher, so I did have an income, if only a small one. Susan was still working as a paraprofessional at a school on Staten Island with special education kids. She loved her job and was great with kids.

We talked about whether we would have kids, but we both decided we would not. Sue was a very nervous person and so was I, and we thought it would be overwhelming for us to try to raise a child. We also made very little money and would be living in the apartment at my

SUSAN

parents' house. My mother supported the idea of us getting married and convinced me that I could get intellectual stimulation from friends and books and that Sue would be a great wife.

We decided to marry the next year. Neither of us wanted a big wedding, so we planned a very tiny but beautiful affair with just immediate family and their spouses and my nephews and nieces. It was on Staten Island at the very classy and supposedly haunted Old Bermuda Inn, with great Italian food that we both loved.

Because I was on Social Security disability, I knew it would be a mistake to have a legal marriage because, per the law, if a person on disability gets married, they lose the check and become the spouse's sole responsibility. I could not survive on the money I made from my part-time job teaching guitar and piano if we divorced and I had to fend for myself. I lived in my parents' house, but they had paid for so many things in my adult life, and they certainly did not need to support me even more. In addition, I could lose my health insurance, and I was on a lot of medicine that I dearly relied on for my sanity.

We decided instead to have a spiritual ceremony conducted by an interfaith minister. We explained the problem to her, and she was very cool with it and said she would marry us under God. She was a wonderful woman who sadly had cancer and was undergoing dialysis, but she was sweet and spiritual and was the perfect person to marry us.

Even after getting engaged, I had my doubts about the whole thing. Years before, after my worst depressive episode, my doctor changed my medication, and I put on seventy pounds. This was horrible for my self-esteem. I felt very uncomfortable with my body, even though Sue told me she loved me just the same. I figured nobody would ever love me like she did, and it was one of the reasons I married her.

We spent the next year planning the wedding and making arrangements. Susan's parents were paying for the affair, and I helped in planning the whole thing. We hired my classical guitar professor to play during the ceremony and the dinner. I was so happy that he would be there, as he had been my mentor and a big part of my life.

My great-aunt was very enthusiastic about the wedding. She loved Susan and thought she would make a wonderful wife for me. I greatly trusted her opinion, as she had been so close to me all my life. She was ninety-four when we got married and unfortunately died very soon after the ceremony.

Sue and I had many things in common. The most important was our spiritual ideals and love of God. We both believed in reincarnation and karma and tried to practice these beliefs in our life.

We each received something of a warning from God to not get married. Sue was very psychic about a lot of things and had a vivid dream in which three old wise women told her not to marry me because it would never work. She told me about it, but we ignored the warnings. On my part, I used to go to an Italian deli all the time and became very friendly with a beautiful young woman who was a cashier there. At one point she asked me out, and I could not believe that such a sweet angel would want to date me. I thought she would have been the perfect woman. I weighed the offer briefly in my mind, and I do think she might have been sent by the angels to help me call off a doomed marriage, but I did not want to hurt my fiancée again, so I said no.

The wedding ceremony was beautiful, and everything went well. It was a rainy day, but everyone had a good time, and we enjoyed the party immensely. We put off our honeymoon at the Mohonk Mountain House until the spring so that we'd have better weather. For the first few months, we got along peacefully, as we always had, and I settled into married life.

Unfortunately, our sex life was not what it used to be. This was primarily my fault. I felt so fat and ugly that I did not even want to take my shirt off in front of her. I wanted to take a big knife and cut my belly off, and my mother did not help by telling me I looked pregnant.

Still, we got along well, although we slept in separate bedrooms because she had to get up early for work and I was a night owl who worked in the afternoons and evenings when the students were home from school. We did lay in her bed a lot to cuddle and watch some TV.

We frequently hung out at Prudence's house with her family and sometimes went out with other couples or by ourselves. We were both content to be around the house or with family. Sue would often go shopping with her mom on Sundays, and I spent a lot of time reading the Sunday sports sections.

I had gotten very big into gardening and cooking during this time, with a lot of influence from my Italian godmother before she died and from Sue's dad. He even helped me plant a fig tree that he took from his garden. I grew so many things and loved to cook everything fresh from the garden.

Things were going okay when I developed intense insomnia for two weeks. I could not sleep and did not know why. Then my two-year-old cat, Chester, threw up green bile, and I knew immediately he was going to die. I realized my insomnia was my subconscious already knowing my baby cat's fate. I told Sue right away that he was dying, but she was doubtful.

I took Chester to the vet, and my worst suspicions were realized. He had cancer, and it had spread all over. He was gone within a week. I was so devastated by this that I cried and cried for weeks, if not months. I loved that cat like a child. He died so young, and I could not wrap my head around it.

I think that was the beginning of the end of our marriage because my heart was broken, and I did not know what to do about it. It was at this point that I started to feel unsatisfied with our married life. I had always wanted to move to a little house on a lake in the Catskills, but I knew Susan would never leave her city job at the school. She also did not want to move away from her family, and she was not a nature person like I was.

Some things bugged me during our marriage. One of them was the laundry. Sue did laundry almost every day and was constantly ironing her clothes. She even said the laundry was her hobby. Even so, she refused to do my laundry. I really did not have much laundry, and I am not so old fashioned that I think a wife should do it, but it seemed strange that she did laundry almost every day and refused to do mine.

Another thing was our cleaning habits. We tried to clean the house once a week, but I ended up doing the entire apartment while she took the whole day to do the small bathroom. She was incredibly slow at it. She did a good job, but what would take me a half hour could take her four. Then there was the fact that I did all the cooking. In addition, she spent more and more time with her mom on the weekends and started to refuse to go to Prudence's house, even though she was my best friend and I loved being there.

I did all the driving as well because she was a very nervous driver and only used her car to get to and from work or to go the few blocks to her parents' house. The main thing, though, was that she had absolutely nothing interesting to say. I was so bored that I was going crazy. We would go to a nice restaurant, and she would just eat and stare at me in silence. This occurred during our dinners at home as well, so I started reading the sports pages while we ate and ignored her. Yes, it was rude of me, but the woman just had nothing to say.

I loved talking to Prudence and to my other friends who were educated. We could discuss intellectual things as well as a host of other topics. Susan almost always talked about her family. She watched the Home Shopping Network all the time and loved Suzanne Somers; hers was one of the few books I ever saw her read. My mind longed for stimulation. I was interested in philosophy, religion, science, technology, history, and so many other topics. I had my books and my friends, but it was not enough. She was driving me to tears. I felt so lonely, even though she was living with me, and I knew I needed to end this horrible marriage.

I dreaded doing it because I knew that I had hurt her before and that this would be a crushing blow because she loved me so much. But there must be more than love to sustain a partnership. I needed someone who could be a real best friend to me and who I could have fun doing things with and talking to. Also, I was not very sexual because of my low self-esteem and weight problem caused by the medications, and I really felt sorry that she was not getting the sex everyone deserves. I finally told her I wanted her to leave, and I made it final. She did not want it to end, and we argued over it. She wanted to go to counseling, but I knew that would solve nothing. I was dying of loneliness while being married, which stopped both of us from trying to find more suitable partners.

I also think she really wanted children and just agreed not to have them because she did not want to lose me. She loved me so much, but I loved her more like a sister now; there was no romantic love at all. She packed her things a few days later, and her family came and took everything that was hers when I was at work.

I came home to an empty house and felt terrible. It was like someone had died. Her family forbade her from ever talking to me again, and our twelve-year relationship and sixteen-month marriage were now officially over.

Susan was a very important person in my life, and we went through so much together. More than anything I respected her as a human being and as a kind, spiritual person. But that just was not enough, so we both moved on.

Chapter 17

MARIA

(1999-2000)

Maria was one of the great loves of my life. She was beyond beautiful both on the outside and on the inside. As stated in the last chapter, I met Maria in the summer immersion program at my college where I was hired for the class as an English tutor.

On the first day, the students wrote essays, and I was to go around and read them all and answer their questions as well as correct their mistakes. I was drawn to Maria right away; she was so remarkably beautiful and sweet. I think I spent at least half the class time working with her, as her dark-brown eyes captivated me, and I could not look away.

After a couple of classes, the students and I were in the hallway chatting, and I began talking with Maria. After a few minutes, I asked if she wanted to go out for a cup of coffee one day. She agreed and gave me her phone number.

We talked on the phone a bit over the next few days, then met at a diner near the college for coffee, as she wanted to take her own car. We had fun and decided to have some food too. I ordered my favorite diner food of French onion soup and grilled cheese. After our meal, I walked her to the car and hugged her goodbye.

For our second date, she came to my house, and we went to the beach. This time she was dressed to kill in tight shorts and makeup. I was blown away because I did not realize she was this hot at the school or on our first date, as she was dressed very casually. She wanted to take separate cars again because she still did not know me that well. Seeing her like this made me realize that I had totally underestimated just how incredibly beautiful she was. Maria was mostly Puerto Rican and had long dark hair and soulful, incredible brown eyes.

She was petite at exactly five feet and weighed about one hundred pounds. I've always loved petite woman; they just seem so adorable to me. I'm not the tallest guy in the world, so we seemed to fit together well.

We went to Great Kills Beach on Staten Island. I spread out a blanket, and we talked for hours. She told me about her life and her great sadness that her brother had died in front of her from diabetes just a few years ago. Maria was three years older than me and had been working for many years as an executive assistant to stockbrokers. She wanted to go back to school to earn her degree and take the Series 7 exam so that she could be a stockbroker too.

She was very smart, and in her time off, she traded stocks on her computer and made enough money to live off. She lacked confidence, though, and did not realize how smart she really was. We sat on the beach and watched the sun go down. We had our first kiss then, which was magical.

We started dating seriously soon after, but I was clear that I wanted an open relationship, and she agreed to that. I was still seeing Susan at the time, so I was very lucky to have two full-time girlfriends during my senior year of college. Dating both of them was great because they fulfilled my different needs, and they complemented each other as my girlfriends.

Maria had an old Chihuahua named Sparky, who had been her brother's dog. He was a mean dog and hated me, but he was so old that he could never catch me to bite me like he wanted to. I would simply run and jump on the couch, where he could not get me.

Maria and I got along well, and I loved being with her. I would write her little notes when I left in the morning, and sometimes I would drive to her house just so that I could hug her good night. Sometimes these hugs would last all night anyway, so we did not get much sleep.

I left her sweet messages on her machine, and she saved them all and would play them back often. I don't think I ever enjoyed cuddling with anyone as much as Maria. She looked so perfect, and I was content to hold her all night. Her skin was so soft, and her naked body was like some kind of rare silk.

Everything was awesome for us. She could cook a little and made me burritos with rice and beans. She always kept on the romantic Spanish stations when we were in bed, and I got to really like that music. I loved the way she spoke Spanish, and she got me into Mark Anthony.

I was learning classical guitar then, and Maria loved for me to play to her. "Spanish Romance" was her favorite, and I played it for her often. A few times when we were lying in bed, I would look at her face and just start weeping. Her beauty was overwhelming to me, and I was falling deeply in love.

Maria was very sensual, as I am, and she told me, "You touch me like I touch myself." She did not mean this in an overtly sexual way; it was just the way my hands moved across her body.

We went out to dinner a lot, as we both loved to go to restaurants, but she was convinced after hearing a silly story that a Chinese restaurant was using cats, so she would never go out for Chinese. I told her that she was being ridiculous, but she was stubborn. Once we had sex in the parking lot of a diner at about ten at night. Afterward, we were driving around, and I dared her to go on someone's lawn half-naked, and she did.

Maria showered twice a day and always smelled wonderful. I used to love to watch her in the shower because she had such a perfect body.

We would play wrestle sometimes in her bed, and she was really strong! I had trouble pinning her arms down, even though I was so much heavier than her. Maria worked out all the time, and she had a perfect line down her back that came only from fitness. She was not to cut up or anything. I don't like girls who are too muscular. I don't find it feminine. Sometimes I would surprise her with gifts, like little teddy bears or balloons at her front door, so that she would find them in the morning when she got up.

We decided to take a vacation together, and I found a place online in the Pocono Mountains in Pennsylvania. It was so cheesy, though, with stupid statues of cupid and hearts everywhere. We both hated it and decided to leave after one night. We had fun anyway and laughed a lot and tried to make the best of the ridiculous place. I was tired on the way back, so she drove my car for a bit, but her bad driving led to a small argument, and we switched back.

Maria had a fantasy about being with a woman. I was all up for that, and we discussed having a threesome. We just needed the right woman to fulfill both our fantasies. She worked with a pretty blonde, but every time I suggested her, Maria would get jealous and mad. We never found the right girl, but looking back I should have just brought her to a strip bar; the strippers would have devoured her.

I graduated from college that spring at the age of twenty-nine, and my parents threw me a big party. Maria wore a yellow flowered sundress that looked so beautiful on her. I still remember it vividly. My friends were all there, as well as many of my relatives, and we had a wonderful time.

One night we went out with a group of my friends to the Cargo Café, and she was kind of quiet. In the car she started crying and said my friends were all so intelligent and she felt so stupid in from of them. I told her that was absurd. She was really smart herself, but for some reason, she lacked self-esteem.

I didn't know what to do after graduation, as I discussed in the last chapter, but I finally got a job working at a bookstore in the mall because I knew the manager from high school. Maria said she was embarrassed to tell her friends that I worked in a bookstore, which I thought was kind of silly, but I despised the job anyway and quit after three weeks.

When something was bothering Maria, she would not argue about it. Instead, she would go completely silent, which I hated. It would take me hours and hours to pull out of her what was on her mind. This was really annoying, but I never wanted us to go sleep angry, so I had to do the work to try to bring out her feelings.

Sometimes she would sleep over, and this was when I was still living in my parents' part of the home. She was embarrassed to be seen by my mom and dad in the morning, even though she was thirty-three years old. My parents liked her a lot, and she got along great with them.

It was around this time that the tenants in my parents' house had to leave because they were running a medical billing business out of the apartment, and it was not in a commercial zone. The city threatened to make my parents pay huge fines, so the tenants had to go. I snatched up this opportunity, and my parents agreed I could move into the apartment.

The apartment had a separate entrance, and I felt I would finally get some autonomy from my family. Maria was not that overjoyed when I happily told her I wanted to live there alone for many years. She wanted us to move in together, and I guess she was thinking marriage, although that subject never came up.

Maria really believed in me and my brain. She used to keep a notebook and write down things that I said that she thought were worth remembering. She even told me that if we got an apartment together somewhere else, I could stay home and write and she would go back to work and pay all the bills. Although this might seem like an amazing offer, I really did not want to live with anybody at the moment. I just loved that apartment.

She wanted to be my only girlfriend and wanted us to stop seeing other people. This was not what I really wanted, but I loved her so much that I thought it was worth a try. The next day I went to Susan's house to tell her that we had to break up and that I was going to be monogamous with Maria. When I got there, her parents were not home, and she had just gotten out of the shower and was in a white robe with her hair all wet.

I had intended to break up with her, but she looked so sexy in her robe and long dark wet hair that I jumped her, and we had amazing hot sex in her bed. So that idea went out the window really fast. I knew I needed to be free then. The next time I hung out with Maria, I told her the truth, not about what had just happened with Susan but that I did not want to settle down at that point. Maria broke up with me, and I was really upset because I loved her truly, but I could not be what she wanted me to be.

The next day I was on an AOL chat room, and I met a girl from New Jersey. She was a young hippie, and we met soon after. We fooled around and hung out for a few days. Eventually Maria and I talked, and I told her about the new girl. She was pissed, but I guess she missed me a lot because we got back together with the same arrangement as before.

We continued to date for a while and then her little dog, Sparky, died. She was inconsolable, and her family had a funeral for the dog the next morning. They'd even built a little casket for him. I missed the funeral because it was very early, and I never really went to sleep until the sun came up. She did not make a big deal of this, but her heart was broken by the death of her beloved Sparky.

Things just got worse from there. She was very different and was just cold. I understood how hard it was to lose a beloved pet, but I could not get her to talk about it. Eventually she broke up with me, this time for good, as she could not give any more of her heart away. She just did not have it in her.

I was really upset and openly cried to a female friend about it. Maria and I decided to stay friends. We hung out at the park one day, and I felt an anger toward her that I'd never had before. We were at her apartment soon after and got involved sexually so we decided to be friends with benefits.

This was an okay situation because I loved being close to her and did not want to let her go. Unfortunately, after a month or so of this,

I made the mistake of being to honest with her and mentioned that I was still seeing Susan. I don't know why, but she snapped. She said that I killed her love and that she never wanted to see me again. I realized I should have kept my mouth shut, but I am a really honest person and don't believe in deceiving people. Nevertheless, that was the last time I saw her.

Maria was truly one of the great loves of my life. I loved her so much and thought I would miss her forever. She had given me a copy of her favorite book, *They Cage the Animals at Night*, about a child going through foster care. She'd written a note at the beginning of the book about what it meant to her. Years later when I was reading the book again, I looked at the back inside cover and saw that she had written a secret note to me that said, "Someday you will belong to someone. Love, Maria and Sparky."

This woman had a profound effect on my life and soul. We were together only about two years, but I will never forget her beautiful face. She was a true romantic and a good person. Her eyes were so beautiful that I can still see them in my mind and know I will forever.

Chapter 18

LEARNING GUITAR

(1996 -?)

When I was twenty-six years old, I decided I wanted to learn to play guitar. My reasoning was simple: I loved nature and all the parks on Staten Island and wanted to bring my music and songbooks to the beach and parks and play and sing. I had a small keyboard, but I hated electric instruments and wanted the pure sound of an acoustic guitar to play in nature.

I began lessons with a young guy at Rustic Music Center not too far from my house. I went there for about four or five months, and I learned the basics. He was a nice kid and a good teacher for someone so young, but I then heard through a friend about a great guitar and lute teacher who was a professor at my school.

His name was Jim Cummings, and the moment I walked into his basement studio and met him, I had a flash that I recognized him from a past life. I was sure I'd known him before. Jim was a great musician and an even better person. He played some classical guitar for me, which was what he played and taught, and I was immediately hooked. I loved the gentle sound of the classical guitar, and I wanted to bring that sound with me to the beauty and serenity of nature.

I had a classical guitar, but it was a piece of crap, so Jim sold me a very good used Angelica classical guitar for fifty dollars. It was a much better instrument and had a sweet sound. I began to learn some classical pieces and how to read the fret board from musical notation. I already knew how to read music from playing the piano, so I had a head start, and the guitar only used the treble clef. The first song I learned was called "Humming" by Ferdinando Carulli. I fell in love with the instrument and with learning the guitar.

Jim was a great guy and was very generous with his time. The lessons were an hour and were inexpensive, and Jim would frequently keep me much longer. We had a great relationship, laughing and kidding around a lot. Those hours I spent with him were some of the happiest of my life. I felt so fulfilled, and I loved to learn.

I was committed to practicing for at least an hour every night. I played scales and his famous page of pain exercises, and I continued to get better. I learned a little folk music and some popular stuff along the way, but the focus was always on the classical technique. I loved learning how to fingerpick; the sound was so beautiful. I remember playing a few times on a bench in the park, and people would tell me how relaxing the sound was.

I was happy learning, and I continued for about a year and a half, until I started to have my heart problems. I was so nervous that I quit the lessons. I could not concentrate on anything at that point in my life. I was so anxious that I couldn't focus.

I stopped the lessons for a couple of years, but here and there I would play the repertoire I had been taught as well as songs from the hundreds of music books I had gathered since childhood. I would play the chords and sing the melody like I did on the piano, though not quite as well.

After my depressive episode in 2001 that I will detail in the next chapter, I started playing guitar with Susan's good friend. He got me excited about music again, and I called Jim and made an appointment for lessons to recommence. I had kept in touch with him over the years after I left, so he knew I had gone through a lot of pain and suffering.

I was so happy to continue my musical education. I still had the music and materials Jim had given me, so we picked up where we had left off. I learned new pieces and different music, even some medieval pieces and Cuban stuff. I truly enjoyed it and was again practicing with great discipline. After about a year of weekly lessons, I decided I wanted to improve my piano playing as well. Again, I had no grand plans for my music or to ever perform for anybody but myself or a girlfriend, but I loved to learn.

Jim gave me his brother-in-law's phone number, and I started piano lessons with him. He was a jazz player, but I wanted to learn classical music. I told him I wanted to play the Chopin études. He laughed and said even he could not play all of them. I'm pretty sure he was kidding about that because he was a phenomenal pianist. Barry was a very tall man with really long fingers, so I could never play the way he did, but I thought I would take lessons for many years and perhaps finally reach my potential. That was my only goal.

Barry gave me a lot of music to work on, including the Clementi sonatinas and pieces by Bach. I asked for my favorite Chopin piece and for "Alla Turca" by Mozart. For as many days of the week I could do so, I practiced piano for two hours and guitar for one hour. Barry was a super brilliant guy, and we had some great conversations. He was a nice dude as well, and it was a pleasure to be his student.

Unfortunately for me, I overdid things, as I am prone to do. I was practicing a part of "Alla Turca" that had an octave part and playing with my left hand. I kept pounding at it over and over again. Pretty soon my hand started to throb with terrible pain between the thumb and index finger. I tried giving it rest and then starting up again, but it did not help; it was swollen and painful. I knew I could not play or practice like I was.

I decided to get medical treatment and went to a famous hand specialist on Park Avenue in Manhattan. Thankfully he took my insurance. He first did an MRI, as he thought there might be a cyst in my hand, but the results came up clean. He diagnosed me with tendonitis and gave me a shot of something into my hand. This helped a little, but when I tried to practice, I knew I could not go on without making it worse. The doctor then prescribed physical therapy. I went for several months, but nothing seemed to help. I was beside myself with sadness and frustration because I had finally found teachers I loved and was making good progress on my instruments, but now everything was fucked.

I was really depressed about the situation and went to talk to Jim. He told me I should teach guitar. I thought this was a crazy idea because I had only taken lessons for a few years and was not an expert. I didn't think I was that good and certainly not qualified to teach anybody else.

This is where Jim saved my life. He told said that I was good enough to teach beginners and that I would learn along the way by teaching. I took this advice to heart, and because I was still recovering from my depressive episode and had no job anyway, I decided to give it a try.

I figured a good way to start was by teaching friends first, and I knew some people who wanted lessons. My Russian friend Olga was my first student. I made up lesson plans and copied music and stuff from books I had. It was during this lesson that something came over me—an intuitive feeling that this was what I was supposed to be doing. I taught another friend too, and they both paid me for their lessons. I had started a new life. I knew I could not play like I wanted to, but teaching gave me something to look forward to and kept me involved in music. Jim had given me more than just the gift of music. He had given me a purpose in life, and he was an incredible mentor. I would call him often with questions about teaching and music and life, and he was such an awesome friend to me.

Eventually I felt comfortable enough to start advertising private lessons in the newspaper, on bulletin boards, and even online. I got my first call from a religious family in the neighborhood who had seen my sign in a kosher restaurant. They wanted me to teach their thirteen-year-old daughter guitar; she was a complete beginner.

We made an appointment for the next week. I prepared a lesson plan and photocopied music, but I was very nervous, as this was my first time teaching a total stranger. I got to the door exactly on time and rang the bell. My heart was pounding in my chest, and I could barely breathe. I did not want her to know that I was a new teacher and that she was my first real student.

Luckily the whole family was very sweet and nice, including Ester, who was a very quiet but extremely intelligent girl. This started me on my teaching adventure, and it saved my life. I loved teaching and always felt happy after each lesson with almost every student. If I was sad or depressed or angry that day, the kids always cheered me up and made me smile. I taught Ester for five years until she went to Israel. She was a great student, and I never came close to not knowing enough to teach her, which was my biggest fear.

I had a lot of wonderful private students for several years. With one religious family, I taught three of their children. The mom was so sweet, and we would talk a lot after the lessons. Her young son was difficult to teach because he would drool all over his and my guitar and sometimes on me; it was really gross. He was a smart kid, though, and I knew he had issues.

His mom told me that he was not doing well in school. The doctor had diagnosed him with ADHD and wanted to put him on medicine. We talked about it, and she was confused about what to do. I broke my cardinal rule about not talking about my history or psych problems and told her that I was on medication and that it had changed my life for the better. Because of this she had her son medicated, and he went through an incredible transformation. Very soon he was one of the best students in his class, and his teachers were extremely pleased with his progress.

In addition, he became a better guitar student, and the drooling stopped as well. I taught those three kids for a long time, and they were one of my favorite families. The mom even shook my hand, which goes against the code of religious Jewish people because men and women are not supposed to touch. She also loaned me a book about cooking vegetarian meals because she knew I was into cooking and was going through one of my vegetarian phases.

I had only a handful of students at any given time, but I finally had a job I could be proud of. It gave me a big boost of confidence because now I could tell people that I was a guitar teacher and not simply a mental patient. I really loved that job, especially because I was working for myself and did not have to deal with a boss.

After several years Jim told me about an opening at Staten Island Music School teaching piano. He thought I would be good at it and offered to recommend me to the boss. He said I would definitely get the job on his word.

I knew it was a great opportunity, but once again I was very nervous because I had never taught piano, though I was a much better piano player than guitar player. I was so nervous because I was completely self-taught. I had only taken those few lessons from Barry and some in high school. I knew that the other teachers at the school were professionally trained and had music degrees. Some were working on their master's. This was very intimidating to me, as I figured I was not in their league.

But I decided to pursue the opportunity and met with the owner. I was really nervous, but on Jim's word, he hired me to fill in for a young woman who was taking maternity leave. She had sixteen students. I was really nervous for many reasons, one being that I didn't know if I had the physical endurance to teach them all back-to-back. I would work two days, with eight students each day for a half hour, one after the other. I would make a lot less than I was charging my private students, but I would make it up in volume. I still had my private students and would teach them on my days off. I had never taught more than three students in a row, so I knew it would be difficult because I was on a lot of medications that made me very tired, and it was hard for me to do a lot of things.

My new career as a piano teacher had begun. I had a tiny studio that was like a big closet and my own piano. I taught from the method books they sold at the school. It was tough because I had to teach them all back-to-back, and I had to meet the parents before and after. I am not a very social person, but it pushed me to make small talk and come out of my shell in order to present myself well to the parents.

As I'd thought, the hardest part was teaching eight kids back-to-back. My medication was very sedating, and I could not drink caffeine because of my heart problem. Although the other teachers were very nice to me, I was intimidated by them because I knew they all had music degrees. My degree was in sociology. I had only taken one music course during my college years, which was a history class.

The kids were amazing and the parents were cool. I knew the owner liked me because we got along really well. He was a nice guy who taught piano and accordion. Some of the students really stood out. One was a Lebanese girl who was smart and funny and really fun to teach. Her mom worked for the United Nations, and she was great to talk to as well.

Another student was an actress who performed in plays and sang. She was always too shy to sing in front of me, but I went to one of her performances in *Fiddler on the Roof*. She was really great and had a wonderful voice. I was so proud of her. She had star quality and a smile that lit up the room.

I had been there for about a year when the young teacher who was out on maternity leave came back. The boss told me he would ask the children if they wanted to go back to her when she returned or stay with me. Fifteen of the sixteen students decided to stay with me, which made me so happy and proud that I was doing a good job and relating well to the kids and their parents.

Unfortunately, and quite tragically, after teaching there for about a year and a half, my doctor took me off my meds, as discussed in a previous chapter. I began to fall apart very quickly, and I quit the job to move to New Paltz. I let all of my private students go as well, and everything I had worked so hard for over the last seven years turned to shit.

Even during my manic episode when I was homeless for four years, I stayed in touch with Jim and would drop by his house when I was in Staten Island. He knew I was sick and homeless and always gave me twenty or thirty dollars for food and would talk with me for a while. His friendship meant so much to me.

I have been stable and well for the past ten years, and I still talk to Jim every couple of months. We laugh and tell stories, and he is a great friend and mentor. He has been a huge positive influence in my life.

Chapter 19

DEPRESSIVE EPISODE

(2001)

By the end of the summer in 2001, I had been working at a retirement community on Staten Island called Island Shores Senior Residence for about a year. I really liked the job and was lucky my boss hired me because I had to disclose my criminal record. She was a sweet woman who was hard of hearing and spoke with a slight accent, but we communicated well.

My job was to be a recreation aide. My duties included showing movies to the elderly residents as well as watching baseball games with the men or taking them on field trips or to the beach. I was mostly hired because I could play the piano, and my boss wanted me to play for the seniors during dinner. It was only a part-time job, but I really loved it. My main task was to talk to the seniors and brighten their day.

They really appreciated that I conversed to them at length and was a good listener. They complained that their family members never visited them. I really enjoyed the work and my time with the seniors. Some of them were really sweet people, and I loved to listen to their stories.

I had been doing well psychologically for many years and was stable on Dr. O'Connor's medicine. My life was going great. I did not tell my boss about my mental illness or the meds I took, but she did openly wonder why I was working only a part-time job there.

Then the perfect storm hit, and my life was again brought into torment. First, the girl I was seeing broke up with me because I only worked part time, and she wanted to get married and have a family and stay home with the children. I had been very secretive with her about my past, and although we'd been dating for three months, she never suspected I was on meds or had a disability. In retrospect, I probably should have been more honest with her.

Still, this hurt me badly, as I was very fond of this woman and thought we had a real future together. Then, at the end of the summer, I was in a very bad car accident, something that had been coming to me in visions for weeks. It finally happened just like I'd seen it in my mind so many times—on the way to the bookstore, a possibly drunk driver hit me head-on and destroyed my car. The driver fled after the accident, and I could have sued him once the police tracked him down. They never charged him with leaving the scene of the accident, though, and this pissed me off.

I hurt my back in the accident, but it was the mental trauma that was the most problematic. I was very calm in the moment and even refused to go to the hospital, but when I woke up the next day, I could barely get out of bed. I was in agony. I went to the doctor, but nothing was broken, just severely bruised, especially my tailbone.

I was in pain for weeks when the biggest blow hit me—the terrorist attack on the World Trade Center. I watched as my two favorite buildings in New York City were hit by airplanes and as thousands of my fellow New Yorkers were killed in front of my eyes. I will never forget that day, as most Americans won't. I didn't know what to do, so I went to my backyard and played Beatles songs on my guitar and tried to make sense of it all.

People with a mental illness are very susceptible to breakdowns after stressful or traumatic events, and a few days later, my life started to unravel. I suffered from terrible anxiety and panic attacks. I started to have seizures again, which had not bothered me for a long time, and would later be diagnosed with epilepsy. I suffered through it and took a Xanax.

Eventually things got so bad that I had to leave my job. I was crushed because I loved that job and was well liked and respected by everyone there. I had really been doing well until these things started to happen.

This was only the beginning, though. I fell into a horrible depression and thought of nothing but suicide for months and months. I seldom left my apartment at my parents' house. I stopped showering regularly and developed all kinds of weird phobias and OCD symptoms. Life had become hell for real. I asked my mom to take me for a lobotomy, and I was dead serious. I did not want to be conscious anymore or be able to think all these horrible thoughts. I did not sleep well, and when I did it was filled with nightmares.

When I woke in the morning after a tortured night of anxiety dreams and barely any sleep, I would throw up. Suicide seemed like my only way out. I thought of many ways to do it, from killing myself with my uncle's M1 Carbine to hanging myself from my favorite tree in the backyard. I devised a plan to visit my uncle and aunt in New Jersey, and while they were in the other room, I'd sneak into their bedroom, find the gun, and end my life. How horrible that would have been for my beloved aunt and uncle and for my whole family.

I could not look at knives because all I could think of was cutting open my wrists. I felt like death was stalking me. I was terrified that I would actually do it and that I would have no control over it. It was like I was on automatic pilot.

I even dreamed about building a guillotine in my backyard and chopping my head off. One day on the way to the mall, I told my father I wanted to kill myself. He replied with this: "I don't know what to say." He was a very quiet man most of the time, and this was very frustrating. I did not have many people to talk to, and all I did was complain and say negative things, so, during this episode, I lost some friends who could not deal with it.

When I talked to my best friend, Ethan, he was really worried about me and said that he thought I was losing every part of myself that made me who I was. My mom could not take the complaining anymore and said that I should go to the mental hospital if I felt that badly. I would not go, though. I did not think there was much they could do for me anyway. One night I was upstairs with my mom and burst into tears. I just lost it and was inconsolable.

My mom said that I never laughed or smiled anymore and that I hadn't for months. The only thing I was interested in was sports. I read the sports pages every day, as I had done since I was a child. I was excited because the New Jersey Nets had a great team and would eventually make it to the championship round that year. I would try to watch funny shows that I had always loved, like *The Simpsons*, but I didn't enjoy anything anymore.

Ethan lived in Long Island now, so I rarely saw him. I had one good friend, Dell, who visited me on the weekends and tried to make me laugh. We sometimes still talk about how fucked up I was then.

The only person I saw regularly was Susan. Although we were just friends now, she came over a few times a week and to hold me in my bed so that I did not kill myself. She really was an angel at heart. My doctor put me on an antidepressant, but I developed an enlarged heart as a side effect of the medication. A sonogram confirmed the diagnosis.

Then came even more horrible symptoms. I started to experience a rare anxious reaction called depersonalization or derealization. Everything began to look weird and funny. It was like there was some kind of frosted glass in front of my eyes, and I could not process visual things like before. I could barely see myself in the mirror. Everything just looked strange.

Dr. O'Connor said there were stimulants to combat depersonalization, but I could not take them because of my previous irregular heartbeats. I felt trapped, like there was no way out of this. I could not believe this was happening to me all at once. I had never experienced anything so horrible before in my life. Just a few months before, everything was going great, and now I lived in a horrible hell world that was literally inside my mind. There was no escaping the emotional and mental pain.

When the doctor took me off the antidepressant, things got even worse. I went back to my cardiologist, and a scan showed that my heart was no longer enlarged. I was thankful for that but now I could not take an antidepressant. I took a Xanax every day at about 4:00 p.m. that made my anxiety better for a few hours.

I was still depressed all the time and wanted to sleep to escape. I stayed on the couch and just existed there for months. I wrote a song about healing, and it seemed to make me feel a little better. It was a prayer to God for my mind to heal.

There were a few things that helped me during this horrible time. I talked on the phone regularly with my therapist. She had moved to Arizona, and my parents were paying for the sessions out of pocket. She was very spiritual and was a good source of positivity. She really thought I would get better, although I could not see through the darkness.

I spoke a lot with my great-aunt, who was also my godmother. She would always tell me, "Don't give up!" She had always been a source of inspiration for me, and I was very close to her. One day I was lying on the couch, and everything changed for a moment. I heard the voice of a women—an angel, I think—who told me I would get better and everything would be all right. This gave me some hope that I would return to normal, despite the terrible symptoms.

Then there was a woman I met on the internet who lived in Connecticut. We talked on the phone almost every day, and she always inspired me. She really liked me and wanted to drive to Staten Island and stay with me for a few days, but I was so sick and anxious that I did not want to see her in person. She mailed me cards and letters all the time, always trying to give me hope and inspiration. We talked so much, and although we never ended up meeting, her sweet personality and kindness in my time of need really helped me.

Two things happened that allowed me to turn the corner. One was that my doctor listened to me, and against his better judgment, he put me back on the meds I had previously been on when I was better. This included Depakote and Risperdal, both of which caused me to put on a lot of weight. I gained seventy pounds in six months, but I started to feel better in the spring.

Springtime was also when I would come out of my seasonal depression, so my natural body cycle worked in my favor. I started to feel less anxious and depressed, and the panic attacks lessened. I was finally able to sleep through the night without terrible dreams.

I started to leave the house and socialize. I went out sometimes with Susan and her best friends. One of her friends was a guy my age who played the guitar. He reinspired me to play music again after hardly touching my instruments for the whole year. We even went on a tour of the Martin guitar factory in Pennsylvania. This was a turning point for me, and we started to play music together all the time. He was a very religious person, and although we had different beliefs, we got along well.

It would be a couple of years before I stopped having any symptoms and got back to normal, but eventually I did. The power of the mind is incredible. I could not believe I had gone through so much pain and so many troubles and had survived without trying to kill myself like I'd attempted to do when I was nineteen. This was the worst depressive episode of my life, and it was caused by the traumas I had experienced in 2001. Because of the car accident and 9/11, I suffered from posttraumatic stress disorder, which obliterated my life for over a year. But I had a good support system, and I believe that my faith in God helped me through and that my constant prayers were answered. I hope those reading this who are experiencing depression, anxiety, or PTSD learn from this that you can get through anything.

Chapter 20

RIKERS ISLAND

(2013-2014)

I had put a deposit on an apartment in New Paltz and was in the process of moving in. My car had been impounded in New Paltz. I had run out of gas, but when a cop came to help me, he found that I was driving without a license and had many tickets to pay. He was nice about it and did not arrest me. He even drove me to a job interview on Main Street at a hamburger joint. Now I had no car, but a friend from town offered to drive me back to Staten Island to get the rest of my belongings.

When we got to the house, I loaded the car and took my new pit bull, who I called Puppy, with us. I'd gotten Puppy for protection because I was still suffering from PTSD from my ordeal in California and was very nervous about things. Puppy was very sweet but was also a great guard dog and made me feel safe.

While I was in the house, the cops rang the bell. I found out later that my mother had gotten a restraining order against me because she wanted me in a hospital. I slammed the door in their faces, and Puppy and I ran up the stairs. I barricaded myself in my sisters' old bedroom. I was able to place a heavy dresser and a mattress between the door and the wall of the closet. It was so secure that it would have taken a bulldozer to get in.

The cops got in the house and were soon screaming at me and banging on the door, but no matter how hard they tried, they could not break the door down. I knew I was eventually going to jail, but I did not want to make it easy for them.

After a long time of trying to break the door down and with Puppy barking like crazy at them, they cut a hole in the wall between my sisters' room and my mother's room. Eventually the lights went out and it got darker in the room, but it was still daylight, so I could see. I hid behind the bed the whole time and smoked cigarettes. I knew that soon I would probably not be able to smoke for a long time.

I had no idea that would be a good year and a half later. I thought of jumping out the window, but the yard was full of cops. I thought of busting my way through the ceiling and into the attic, but that would have just stalled the inevitable. Eventually they cut a big hole in the wall and shined their laser-pointed weapons through the bedroom.

When they said they were going to shoot Puppy if I did not open the door, I knew I had to give myself up. I tied up the dog as they asked me to and then told them to be calm and that I was unarmed. I opened the door, and they grabbed me and put me in cuffs. The house was filled with police in full riot gear. They took me outside, where tons of neighbors watched the scene unfold. I screamed at them as they put me in an ambulance.

Our first stop was a mental hospital on Staten Island. I was still screaming, so they cuffed my hands and feet to a chair. They tried to give me a shot of some kind of tranquilizer, but again I was not going to make it easy for them and continued to spit in the face of the male nurse who was trying to sedate me. They put a pillowcase over my face so that I would not spit on them or bite them. I kept moving my shoulder violently so that he could not give me the shot. He eventually got it in, and my arm was severely bruised for weeks after the struggle.

They eventually took me to Bellevue Hospital Prison Ward 19 West in Manhattan, where I stayed for about a week, until an officer came to my room and said, "Get your stuff together. They're sending you to Rikers." This was scary. Rikers has been described as the worst and most notorious jail complex in the United States. I had heard the stories and knew I was in for some serious trouble.

I knew I would have to fight while there, and my biggest fear other than that was that I would have to become an animal to survive and that I would lose my humanity. I am at heart a gentle and kind person, but I knew I would have to shut that part of me down to make it out in one piece.

When they first put me in there, I had to go through a processing phase that took about four days. I was put inside a small cage with about ten other inmates, and we had to sit mostly on a cement floor. There was only one open steel toilet for all of us. A couple of guys were smoking something, and I asked for a hit. I don't know what it was, but it made me tired.

A man standing next to me had a grand mal seizure and started shaking violently. As he fell to the floor, another inmate grabbed his hand and pulled the rings off his fingers. The man having the seizure smashed his head on the steel toilet, cracking it open. There was blood everywhere, and I thought he was dead. Eventually they put him on a gurney and took him away. That was my welcome to Rikers Island.

The next day we were put into a larger room that held about a hundred inmates all lying on a cement floor with no blankets or pillows. Some people used newspaper or pieces of cardboard for their heads. They fed us three really bad meals a day, and there were only two toilets for a hundred men and no privacy. I was there for three more days and then they brought us through an X-ray machine to check for weapons and made us strip and spread our butt cheeks to see if we had drugs or weapons in there.

Eventually I was taken to a dorm with about forty other inmates. I tried to keep to myself and deal with the new situation. One night they woke me at about 3:30 a.m. and told me I was going to see the judge. They took me to the area where the buses leave for Staten Island and the other boroughs to go to court. I saw a lot of fights between gang members. The corrections officers called it fight club.

At the courthouse in Staten Island, I waited in a cage with a lot of other men to see the judge. They gave us sandwiches; some cheese and some peanut butter and jelly. I hate peanut butter but love cheese, so I had to be aggressive to get the cheese sandwiches.

After waiting all day, I finally saw the judge, but my lawyers said it did not go well. I was still manic and pissed off that I was taken there, and I screamed at the judge. I was jumped by a bunch of court officers who dragged me back to the holding cell. Eventually I was handcuffed to another inmate and put on the bus for the long drive back to Rikers.

There I had to go through almost the whole intake process again, sitting on the cement floor and waiting for days to be put back in a dorm. I applied for a job so that I would have something to do, but because I was officially under mental observation, which meant that I was put in with the criminally insane, I was not eligible to work.

I talked to my mother on the phone, and she put money in my commissary account so that I could get chips, coffee, and other snacks. This was really important, as the food was horrible and made everyone even more irritable. I couldn't get cigarettes because of the new laws against smoking in jail, and I did not want to get involved with people who were selling contraband tobacco in the jail because I did not want to owe anyone anything.

I smoked something with a guy in the dorms and being delusional, I thought he gave me drugs, instead of what he called tea. Looking back, we smoked the contents of a tea bag from the commissary, but I was quite paranoid. I confronted him that night and told him I wanted to fight him in the bathroom. Another guy jumped me, and I fell over the beds. A screaming match and chaos ensued. They threw me out of that dorm and put me in with the worst and craziest patients in the jail. They tried to intimidate me and threw apples and other things at my head. I talked to the captain, and he took mercy on me and had me transferred again.

Being manic meant I couldn't sleep at night, so the officer in charge let me pace the new dorm while the others slept. I wanted something to do and asked to go to Jewish services on Friday nights with a few other Jewish prisoners to see the rabbi. To go to Jewish services, you must have the word *Jewish* on the ID card that you are supposed to wear all the time. Every person had their religion printed on their IDs. I had mine switched, but they informed me that I couldn't eat the regular meals now. I would have to eat the kosher ones if I claimed to be Jewish.

Some of those meals were okay, but they were very small portions, and I was quite hungry and was more willing to eat the crappy Rikers regular food. At first, they gave me what I wanted but then one night I tried to get my meal in the dinner line, and a big Italian guy said that this was what Jews have to eat. He tried to give me a tiny cardboard box with a stinky little fish in it. I hate fish and was not going to eat it, so I tossed it back onto the counter through the kitchen door cutaway.

The Italian guy opened the door quickly, and I thought he was going to argue with me, as he'd been a former friend before this, but instead he sucker punched me in the head with a huge roundhouse right. My glasses went flying off, and I closed my eyes tightly because I was afraid of getting cuts on my eyes from the glass. It was probably the hardest I ever had been punched, but I went straight at him and started hitting him with lefts and rights to his head. Eventually they pulled me off him. I finally opened my eyes and saw that he was on the ground. I screamed at him that I was going to kill him. He yelled something back, but I knew I had won the fight. Then about a million officers came running in and took me away in handcuffs. Apparently, a riot had broken out over the fight, with the inmates taking different sides. As a team of guards hauled me off to a holding cell, another team of riot guards headed toward the cellblock. I continued to scream the whole way to the cell.

Eventually I was transferred to another cellblock, this one again for the criminally insane. Some people there screamed all day and others were heavily medicated. At least there was group counseling in this cellblock, so there was something to do, although it was too early in the morning. Some people played board games or cards, but I was not interested in this. Instead, I tried to read some books that I had.

My lawyers finally got in touch with me and said they were getting me out to a three-quarter house, where I was mandated by the court to stay and attend a MICA program. This was absurd because I had not been addicted to drugs in more than twenty years, but that was where the judge wanted me.

For my day in court, the head lawyer of the defense team was very kind to me and drove me all the way to Brooklyn, where the three-quarter house was. We talked a lot, and he even bought me pizza. The house was a real hellhole and not much different from the jail. It was also in a dangerous neighborhood.

To make matters worse, I had no money and there was no food available. I had no cigarettes either, and I was dying to smoke after five months in jail. The person in charge gave me a couple of dollars to get some cookies or something, but I was starving because I had not eaten much all day. I did manage to get a cigarette from someone, but I was there manic and penniless. The next day we were going to apply for food stamps, but it could take days to get them, and I had no idea how I planned to eat in the meantime.

That night I said, "Fuck this!" I snuck on the train back to Manhattan and walked to the Staten Island Ferry. By that time, it was about three in the morning, and none of the buses were running, so I walked the eight or nine miles to the Social Security office near the mall to try to get my check turned back on. I had no ID, so I was homeless and penniless again, but at least I was in a place that I knew well and where I could survive.

I stopped at my friend Ethan's uncle's house and asked if he could help me, as he and his family had known me almost all my life. Ethan's uncle really saved my ass that night. It was raining heavily, and my feet were soaking wet. He gave me some sneakers and a wallet, and he put about thirty-five dollars in it. I was able to walk to the nearby Z-One Diner for some food and to get out of the rain. I got my favorite, French onion soup, and I was happy to be out of Rikers and still alive.

They knew me at Z-One, as I had been going there for years. The manager let me sleep in the back in an empty booth. He was so nice to me, and I was glad I had these friends to help me.

The next day I walked a couple of miles to the shrine at the Society of Saint Paul, where I knew I could sleep and nobody would bother me. After staying there for a couple of nights, I ran into my old friend Nancy at the 7-Eleven down the block. We talked and she knew I was homeless. We had originally met through my mom because she was my mom's hairdresser. She had done my hair too a few times. Nancy gave me about forty dollars, and I used the money to go back to New Paltz where I knew I would be safe.

I took the bus to the ferry to the train and then paid twenty-three dollars for the bus ticket to New Paltz, which was my favorite place on Earth at that time. I was looking forward to getting back there. I got food from the New Paltz food bank, saw my old friends, and met a musician who let me crash at his house for a few days. We jammed together during an open mic night, and I sang "The House of the Rising Sun" while he played guitar.

New Paltz was a universe away from the hell of Rikers Island. It was situated in the beautiful mountains, and the people were sweet and generous. It was like returning to heaven after five months in hell. I knew I was home. I used somebody's cell phone to call the courthouse in Staten Island, and I cursed out the judge for putting a mentally ill man in Rikers and for putting me in a MICA program when I was not a drug addict.

It probably was not a good idea to tweak the judge's beak that way. Even though I now had a warrant out for leaving a program, I figured they would just leave me alone for something so stupid. I was very wrong about that. After a few of weeks of being in New Paltz, a couple of police cars approached as I was exiting a record store. They knew who I was and told me they were bringing me back to Rikers Island. I was upset and still manic. I asked the cops if I could smoke a last cigarette before they hauled me in. They let me.

Back at Rikers, it was the same deal: days spent in intake on the cement with hundreds of other men waiting for the X-rays and strip searches. This time they put me in a general population cellblock with mostly gang members. I found it much better than the so-called mental observation units. These guys were cool, and I made a very good friend there who told me to call him Arthur. Arthur was in his twenties and looked out for me all he could.

The guys in the cellblock I was now in tried to help me because they knew I had mental problems. They would try to get me to go to my medical appointments and to take my medications.

I mostly stayed in my cell to sleep or do my mantras, but Arthur always tried to get me to hang out with them. I was just not that social. Even when I had my commissary money stolen by Rikers for all my infractions or rebellions, some of the guys would work out a deal with me where my mom would put the money in their account, I would give them a list, and they would get my food and coffee. In return, I gave them some of the money for themselves. It was a fair deal and nobody ever tried to screw me over.

The security in the cellblock was very tight because it was for very violent or bad criminals. Often the guards made us get naked in our cells and spread our butt cheeks, sometimes in front of female personnel, and have all our things X-rayed. They would come in with huge German shepherds to check our cells.

One time when they had us all lined up against the wall while they searched our cells, I screamed three times, "Who do you think you are?" The gang member next to me tried to make me be quiet because he knew I could get a beating from the guards for opening my mouth like that.

Every once in a while, they would put plastic cuffs on us behind our backs. One time it was so tight that my wrists bled. Then they would take us by bus to the medical building to have a full body scan to check for drugs or weapons inside of us. This could take all day, and with the plastic cuffs behind our backs that were so tight that they made me bleed, I felt like I was being tortured.

The only real fight I had in this cellblock was one I started myself. Even though I was taking medication, it was not working, and I was still quite manic and paranoid. I thought the dude in the cell next to me had raped my girlfriend. I really believed it, even though I had completely made it up inside my head. I jumped him in the dinner line and tried to wrestle him to the ground in a headlock. Arthur knew the guy had not done anything to me and pulled me off him. I went back to my cell but was still screaming at the guy and tried again to attack him. I attempted to climb over a steel wall to get at him, and when Arthur pulled me down, I shattered my big toe.

The toe hurt me for months, but I never got treated for it. I just ignored it because I don't think they could have done anything anyway except perhaps tape it. To show you that everyone is not evil in jail, I was able to make peace with the guy I jumped. A few days later, I approached him and apologized. I told him I had mental problems and said I was sorry. He said he knew it was my disease that caused the attack, and he replied, "Notice that I did not retaliate." He could have too. There was nothing stopping him from jumping me back or getting me shanked. That shit went on all the time at Rikers. I saw somebody get stabbed earlier in my stay.

On one occasion I was sent to court, but the judge refused to see me. The process started in the middle of the night, where I watched the gang fighting in the waiting area by the buses. It was a long tortuous day of going to Staten Island and back from Queens. In the waiting area, a huge muscular guy came in and began screaming at the other inmates. His fist was balled up in a punching position. He was looking for rival gang members, and all forty or fifty of us backed up in fear of this man.

He went to the smallest guy there and punched him in the head three times, making a loud thud, thud, thud. The small guy was bleeding from his face and tried to hide behind the toilet. Eventually the corrections officer got the little guy out of there and put the huge strong man in another holding area, but it made a lasting impression on me. Everyone was afraid of this man.

When it because obvious that I was not going to see the judge that day, even though I'd gone through all the annoying bullshit to get there, I was pissed and screamed at the court officer. He cuffed my hands behind my back and my feet together and then dragged me to the bus. I tried to make it hard for him by lifting my cuffed hands up behind me, I then spit right into his face. He threw me into the seat, then took my head and smashed it against the metal bus wall. I felt a strange sensation like I was bleeding, but it was on the inside of my head. Then he punched me in the face. I never told my lawyers about it because I knew there was no proof and nothing I could do. That was just Rikers.

About a month later, I went to court again. This time I saw the judge, and my lawyers and the district attorney decided I had been locked up long enough and were going to release me. The judge was against it and said he could not believe they were going to release me to the streets, but because both my lawyers and the DA agreed, he allowed it.

I served eleven months in the worst jail in the country, what is called a Rikers year. I had never been convicted of a crime of any kind. I was just housed there like an animal. I survived with the help of God and my wits. I am still afraid of going back there. It's haunted me for a long time. It was so fucked up that at times I thought I was already dead when I was in there and that I was in purgatory or hell.

I was released in February, and it was only fourteen degrees outside, but I was now free, although I was still homeless and penniless. I knew I would have to survive on the streets again, but I felt nothing but pure joy and happiness. I would rather be homeless any day than spend more time in that hellhole. I was free at last.

Chapter 21

AFTER RIKERS

(2014)

After my release from Rikers Island, I walked from the courthouse to the bus stop and asked the driver if he could take me for free. He agreed and brought me to my old neighborhood. I met my mom's housekeeper, and she gave me a blanket and some money from my mom and most importantly the key to my storage facility on Forest Avenue.

I found all my stuff that had been kept there for years and paid for by my mom. I enjoyed going through my things, which included my computer and all kinds of clothes. I was overjoyed and put on three pairs of socks, three undershirts, another pair of jeans, and a winter coat, a hat, and gloves. I tried to sleep in the storage box, but they somehow knew I was there and kicked me out at night.

I know Staten Island like the back of my hand, so I went into some woods I was familiar with, thinking it would be safer there. I slept on the snow underneath my blanket. I was still cold, but I knew I could survive now. I woke the next day to find that water and snow had gotten into my boot; my right foot was frozen solid. I went into a Burger King to warm up, and they let me sit there for as long as I liked. I took my boot off and was able to thaw out my foot. By some miracle I did not have frostbite.

During the day a bus driver let me sit with him on the bus while he was on a break to get out of the cold. I really can't say enough good things about the New York City bus drivers during my ordeal. They always let me ride for free when I was broke, and they were always kind to me. I don't know what I would have done without their help. They truly saved my ass because it was the only way I could get around without money.

After a few days, a lot of people helped me. I was near a deli one day and told the owner that I did not have money or food. He said he would make me a hot sandwich of anything I wanted. I ordered a big hero of roast beef and cheese, and it was the best thing I had eaten in years. Don't ever believe that there are not good people out there because there absolutely are.

I made my way back to the Alba House on Victory Boulevard with the outdoor shrine that I liked to sleep in. The candles kept me warm at night, and I felt safe there in my old neighborhood. One day when I was hanging out there, two older women started talking to me, and I told them about my situation. They said they did not have much, but they gave me thirty dollars to get home to New Paltz. That was the only place I wanted to be, and those two angels made it possible.

Once again, I took the bus to the ferry to the subway to the port authority bus terminal and paid twenty-three dollars for a bus ticket to New Paltz. Once there I started living in the twenty-four-hour Laundromat again and hanging out with my friends and the kids from the college. I was having fun and enjoying my freedom and my favorite town and people when I went into a bank to ask some questions about an account. I was very confused and manic, and they realized I needed psychiatric help. While I was there, the police and an ambulance showed up and took me to a hospital for observation. Although I was sad and upset at the time, they really saved my life because this would get me back on the right meds and free to live a normal life again.

They put me in Saint Mary's Hospital in Kingston, New York, and although it was not a bad place, I still hated to lose my freedom. The food was excellent, and eventually they gave me my own room. The person who really saved my life, though, was the psychiatrist who realized I was not getting better on the meds they were giving me. He asked what I'd been taking when I was stable. I told him it was Mellaril, an older medication. He said they didn't use that anymore because it could cause heart problems, but he decided to try an older related medication called Prolixin. This was like a miracle for me, and I got back to my sane stable self. Finally, after four long years of hell and torture, I was going to be okay.

I was in the hospital for six weeks before being released to a nearby rooming house. There I could smoke in my room and received three meals a day in exchange for a small portion of my disability check. Unfortunately, I was having a lot of trouble turning on my SSD check. The social worker at the hospital was supposed to have done it, but it did not go through.

The owner of the rooming house was a huge man—easily seven feet tall—and it was not very long before he told me he hated me. I was not getting paid yet because I did not have my check turned on, and he was constantly having to lend me money to buy food and stuff. I had told him once to go fuck himself, so maybe that did not sit too well with him.

What really screwed me up was the fact that when I left the hospital, they did not give me a professional social worker to deal with but a peer advocate. This young man drove me to the rooming house, and first we stopped at CVS to drop off my prescriptions. We did not have enough money to pay for them, and this was when the real trouble began.

About a week later, I started to get manic again without the meds. One day I was walking around the town looking at the shops and cafés when, on my way home to the rooming house, I noticed there was an ambulance in the driveway. I immediately thought they were there to take me back to the hospital. I kept walking down the road and into the mountains. I stopped at a small diner on the way, where the owner gave me something to eat, and then I continued down the highway. Eventually I came to another town with a bus station. I wanted to get on the bus to Woodstock because I knew that there was a Tibetan Buddhist monastery there and that they would help me find a place to sleep and give me food.

Someone in the town hall who I talked to gave me money for the bus ticket and said I could pay it back someday. I took the bus to Woodstock, and it was already getting dark when I got there. I knew the monastery was way up in the mountains, so I started walking along the main road to the Tibetan place. I came to a fork in the road and was confused about which one to take because I had been walking for quite a while.

I must have taken the wrong road because I never found the monastery, but I came to a huge private property and went through a hole in the fence. It was a beautiful place with a stream, greenhouse, and pool, along with a very expensive house. Here is where my mental illness kicked in, and I decided that the house was for me. I mean, I really believed it was my house. Even though I had an intuition that there was an alarm system, I still used a rock to break a window.

Within seconds, an extremely loud alarm sounded, and knew I was fucked. The police arrived in minutes. I tried to hide in the attic and thought maybe they would think I had left the house. Unfortunately, they brought a K-9 unit with them, and the dog started barking, so they knew I was there.

I was hiding in the back of the attic when the door to the stairs burst open, and a lot of cops came in screaming at me with their weapons drawn. I told them I was unarmed and came out of my hiding spot. They jumped me and handcuffed my hands and feet. One officer also tried to tase me three times for no reason. I heard the click, click, click as he pressed the taser to my side, but God was with me that day because it failed to go off.

They carried me down from the attic and threw me in the back of the squad car. I was manic and angry and yelling at the cop. He told me he would shoot me if I did not shut up.

They brought me to the local jail. I saw the judge, but I turned my back on her and would not speak. By my actions, they knew I was obviously not sane. Later I was taken to Ulster County Jail and put in an isolation room in some kind of weird suit so that I would not commit suicide. I don't know why they put me there. I was not suicidal, but I guess that was their procedure.

Finally, I started taking my meds again—the right ones—and within days I was back to my old sane self. My mom had glasses sent to me and everything changed for the better. I could actually see that the psychiatrist at the jail was someone I knew from the hospital.

This place was jail, but it was nothing like Rikers Island. It was like Disneyland compared to Rikers. The food was still shit, but basically everyone got along. I saw only one fight in the six weeks that I was there. The best thing was that you could get food from outside the jail through the commissary. My mom was nice enough to again put money in the commissary for me.

The most important thing was that I had a social worker take on my case. She worked with the lawyers, and the judge dropped the charges. She wanted me to go to South Beach Psychiatric Center in Staten Island because she knew I would get the best treatment there.

After spending six weeks in jail, a couple of the corrections officers drove me back to Staten Island to get the help I needed. That social worker and judge treated me so well; they knew I was not a criminal but a sick person. And for that I will forever be in their debt.

I was so happy to be going back to South Beach Psych. As the officers drove me down, I thought of how well I knew so many people there and that I would finally be out of jail. Nobody likes to be locked in a hospital, but there I had friends, knew a lot of the staff, and my mother had worked there as a special education teacher on the adolescent unit for over twenty-five years.

I had been there as a young person to visit my mother at her job, and I had been interred there many times to get better. When the officers brought me to the unit I was to be held in, I was greeted by the familiar face of a therapist I knew very well. He said I was just a little manic and would probably be out in five or six weeks. The officers took off the handcuffs, and I felt freedom again. That was ten years ago, and I have not been in handcuffs since.

I had to stay on the unit for a few days for observation. I met my new therapist, a pretty young social worker who was very kind to me and seemed to care a lot about her patients. After a few days, I was allowed to go down to the lunchroom with the other patients for my meals. Just being in a room without armed guards and dangerous people was such a happy thing for me.

I decided that first week that I was not going to fuck things up this time. I made a promise to myself that I would follow every rule and direction and do everything the doctors and nurses and therapist said. I was determined to get my life back to normal. They asked me to take the Prolixin by injection every week, and I agreed. They told me the injectable worked better than the pills, and I was not going to argue with them.

I was back on Depakote as well. They tested my blood levels a lot, but I would never argue and always let them do what was needed. I showered and shaved every morning, even if I was tired from the meds, because they told me it was important. I wanted to get out as soon as possible, so I followed every direction they gave me.

After a few days, I started going to another building with other patients for programs. The campus was beautiful, and I liked getting out and going for a walk. South Beach Psychiatric Center is also a state preserve for wild turkeys. They were quite humorous and were everywhere, running, flying, and trying to get any food you had.

At the programs building, there was a piano I could play and even a guitar that they would take out of a closet for me. They offered several different groups, from music to art therapy to educational classes and other stuff. But the best thing about the program was that I found my old girlfriend Geneva. Geneva was beautiful. She looked a lot like Katy Perry in every way, with long dark hair and large radiant green eyes. Geneva was a Sephardic Jewish girl with roots in Syria. She was very smart and fun and could speak five languages.

She had a reputation for being very promiscuous, but that did not bother me because she and I had a special bond. During the groups we often spent our time together cuddling up and holding hands. It was so wonderful to be with a beautiful woman again, and I still loved her deeply.

After about ten days there, they gave me grounds privileges, which meant that every day for a couple of hours I could be out on my own and just hang out on campus or go to the cafeteria. They had great food at the cafeteria, and I would frequently get grilled cheese sandwiches, which were awesome. The best part of grounds privileges was that I could smoke in certain areas of the campus where there were no cameras. Even better, I could buy cigarettes through the gate where people came to sell them and then I would sneak them inside the building and smoke them in the bathrooms.

My mom gave me some money so that I would have things there. I hung out with Geneva not only during the programs but also sometimes during grounds privileges.

One of my favorite activities to do at South Beach was art. I would use watercolors to paint lots of flowers and other things, or I would use a pencil to sketch pretty women from fashion magazine. Sometimes Geneva and I would do art together.

Her favorite thing to do with me at the program was to go to the women's group where they did one another's nails and chatted and listened to music. They let me hang out there with her, and she loved to hold my hands and buff my nails and have fun with me.

Eventually they told me I was getting out soon. I interviewed with a woman on the campus who was in charge of the housing program. This program was great, and they agreed to set me up in a beautiful modern apartment with a roommate but with my own bedroom. It was just down the street from the hospital, so I could walk to see my therapist and doctor.

I was working with a new therapist on the ward, and he knew I was in a rush to get out and be on my own again, this time on the right medication. Then I would be completely sane and back in Staten Island where I grew up and knew everybody. He was so nice that he spent his whole weekend working at home on the forms so that I could leave the next week. It was an extremely joyous occasion the day I was to go to my new home off Hylan Boulevard, where there was so much great food that I loved and where I had spent my whole life nearby.

We packed up my stuff in large brown bags, and my new therapist drove me down the block to my beautiful new home where I was to start my new life. Thank you, South Beach Psychiatric Center, the state of New York, and everyone who contributed to giving me my life back.

Chapter 22

LIVING IN STATEN ISLAND AGAIN

(2015)

The beautiful apartment was on the second floor. It was a modern building with a washer and dryer in the basement. It had two bedrooms, and the larger bedroom included a balcony overlooking the front of the building. My roommate had the big bedroom, and they set me up in the smaller one with a new bed and furniture.

My roommate, Jack, was Korean and also played the guitar and liked sports. I guess they figured we had that in common and would get along. He was a nice enough guy in his mid-thirties while I was forty-four. Jack had a rule to take our shoes off at the door, which was a

Korean thing, but that was no problem for me. Jack was also a born-again Christian and a virgin who went to church in Manhattan every Sunday. He was saving himself for marriage apparently.

The rent was 30 percent of my check, so I had enough money to live and be free. Of course I was very poor, and this is where my mom helped me out so much once again. She bought me a laptop and new clothes and a cell phone. I was a normal human being again and could get online and watch YouTube and access everything that a smartphone could do.

I reunited with my family who I had not spoken to in years and reached out to some friends as well. The best part of living on my own again was that Geneva was in an outpatient unit on the grounds of South Beach, so she could come by and sleep over whenever she wanted.

Sleeping with her was beautiful. I loved to watch her take showers while I admired her sexy body. Having a sex life again was wonderful, and I loved her dearly. She was a fun person and supersmart and intuitive. Sometimes after we went to bed, I would glance at her under the covers. It gave me such a warm, safe feeling to have her next to me.

With a little of the extra money I had, my mom took me to Guitar Center in New Jersey, and I bought a Cordoba classical guitar with a pickup and a small acoustic amplifier. I also had some of my stuff from storage and from my mom's house, so I set up my old Casio keyboard and music in the living room. I had music again. I could play it and listen to all my favorite artists on YouTube. The phone was an android and had special speakers on the back to amplify the sound.

The neighbors were okay, but some dude on the third floor complained about me singing and playing through my amp, so I could not do that anymore, but I could sing and play acoustically. Jack played his guitar in the living room, but it was mostly the Christian stuff he loved.

I had a therapist at an outpatient building at South Beach, and she was awesome. She always had my back and helped me out all the time. She was also a professor at the College of Staten Island, and I must admit I had a huge crush on her the whole time.

One of the great things about being free and living in Staten Island again was the food. I loved to get Italian food or Chinese or Mexican, which was everywhere, and of course the great New York City delis, where I could get a sandwich any time of the day or night. My favorite was roast beef and cheese, which I got a lot from the Italian deli down the block. When you have been homeless or in jail or in a mental hospital, you don't take for granted all the little things that make life wonderful. Just being able to take a shower in a private bathroom that I shared with one person made me so grateful. It was wonderful.

My aunt and uncle visited, and they gave me a flat-screen television. Jack and I split the cable bill. Everything was amazing. I had my own room and my own television and my instruments. I had books to read and would get the newspaper a lot for the sports sections. Jack was a Yankees fan, but I got to watch my beloved Mets whenever I wanted. When everything is taken away from you, they mean that much more when you get them back.

My mom stepped up yet again, and we started working on getting my driver's license back. I had a suspended license and many tickets from when I was manic, so with lots of time and working with the DMV, my mother paid $2,400 to get my license back. Then she went further and let me use her car for the winter until she came back from Florida, when she bought me an inexpensive old Toyota Camry. The car was kind of falling apart, but it worked and it was a Toyota, so it probably would run forever.

Geneva and I had basically an open relationship. She told me that she did not care what I did with other women but that she did not want me to tell her about it. I knew she was with other men as well because on occasion I would see her walking hand in hand with some blond dude. I loved Geneva, but I knew she was not the permanent solution to my love life, so I dated others. Geneva was a sweet person, but she had schizophrenia and was very much way out there. I tried to help her as much as possible, but her personality was very erratic.

Now I had a car, a clean license, a nice apartment, and a girlfriend. I really had everything anyone could want. I was back to seeing my family on the holidays, and I even made a new friend in the building named Abraham. Abe lived down the hall with his girlfriend, and Jack would take me over there sometimes to hang out. Abe was thirteen years younger than me, and we became good friends. He would come to my place almost every night, and we would smoke cigarettes and talk in my room. We were not supposed to smoke in the apartment, but I had set up a fan facing out the window to try to ventilate as much as possible.

One day I met Millie on the grounds of South Beach, where I had a pass to come and go whenever I wanted. Millie had been in my programs when I was in the hospital, and I liked her a lot. She was a religious Jew and always had on a long skirt. She was a little chubby, but I loved her beautiful blue eyes and personality. I asked her to get coffee with me, and she agreed.

On our date she said that she had a boyfriend in Brooklyn but that she really liked me. The next time we hung out was at my apartment. I kissed her, and she laughed and said, "Don't tell my boyfriend." Millie was religious, so she was waiting for marriage to have sex, but we fooled around a little. We had lots of fun together and went out to eat a lot and walked in the parks. She was much saner than Geneva, and I enjoyed her company. She was into women as well, and we had fun once going to a strip bar together.

The funny thing is that both Geneva and Millie lived in the same building on the grounds of South Beach, and they did not like each other at all. Millie and I tried to keep our relationship a secret from Geneva, but she found pictures of her in my phone and knew something was going on. Millie was most likely afraid of Geneva, as she had a reputation of being violent sometimes. She never hit me or even came close to that; I think it was mostly other girls she would get into it with.

Now I had two girlfriends and a car and an apartment and a little money, and things were going very smoothly until my roommate decided to stop taking his medication and flipped out on me. We took turns cleaning every other Saturday. It was my day to clean, but he did it for me anyway and then decided to eat the food that my mom had bought me at the grocery store.

Having been homeless, I was very sensitive to people eating my food. I told him not to touch my food without asking first. We got into an argument and then I felt bad later that night and offered to buy him some Italian food I was getting delivered. He said no, but the next morning when I woke up, he was gone but had trashed all my stuff. He threw away my glasses and ripped up my book and broke my amplifier and lots of others malicious acts.

Then I got a call from the woman who ran the program. She told me Jack had come to her office and told her he could not go home. I agreed with that statement because I was really pissed. He was shipped off to the mental hospital, and I had the apartment for myself for a while. I neatly packed up all of his stuff and took over his room so that I could have the balcony to smoke on and play my guitar outside.

Eventually they gave me a new roommate. I'd met him before, and he was a really cool guy. I liked him way better than Jack, and we got along great. He spent a lot of time sleeping, but when he got up, he always asked me if I needed anything when he went to the store. John was very into video games and action figures, and he had a roomful of them still in the boxes. He was a collector.

John was a good cook as well and always offered me food. He made the best garlic mashed potatoes and other stuff. We really got along well, and all was peaceful.

I was enjoying the way my life was going now and felt very serene and mentally balanced. I decided to look for a part-time job in the neighborhood. I applied at the pet store down the block, but they wanted my driver's license and Social Security numbers, so I knew they were going to check my criminal record. They never called back, even though I'd had a very positive interview with the owner.

Now that I had a car, I thought I would go back to teaching piano and guitar to kids, since that had been the best job I'd ever had. My uncle came through big-time and helped me with this. He was good friends with a printer who lived in Staten Island. My uncle told him what I had gone through, and he was kind enough to put out an advertisement in one of the local papers he printed and would place it there every week for free. On top of this kindness, he made up a box of business cards for me using a logo and design I came up with.

Advertising would have been expensive, but it was the only way I could get my business going again. The fact that this was done for me for free tells you of the big hearts that some people have. After a few months, I had a couple of students, and I was back in the game. I had all my materials at my storage bin and at my parents' house, and I was happy to be earning a few dollars on my own again.

One of my students was an autistic teenage boy. He wanted piano lessons and had already been taking them for a few years with another teacher. He was a nice kid, and his family was wonderful. The mom was so sweet and kind, and the dad was a really talented artist and musician. He was a sanitation worker and used to collect all kinds of instruments and amplifiers he found and rebuild them.

Another student was an eleven-year-old blond boy who was not keen on piano lessons, but his parents and grandmother insisted. He was very bright, though, and picked it up quickly. He liked for me to play a song and sing it at the end of the lesson, which became our routine.

Unfortunately, at about that time, I started having seizures again. My eyes would start twitching underneath my eyelids, and it was really disconcerting. I told my psychiatrist at the outpatient clinic where I got my meds and therapy, and she said to take a video when this happened. I did that, but she had no idea what it was. I even went into a seizure when I was watching my roommate play video games.

My mom kept telling me to go to a neurologist, something I had resisted for years. Now I decided to make an appointment and have it checked out, even though I had thought for years that it was just a weird panic attack.

The doctor talked to me for a long time and did a lot of testing, including an EEG, and she told me I had epilepsy. She explained that seizures could be quite large or even the smallest thing and that it was coming from the brain. Having used Klonopin or Xanax to treat it made sense now because she explained that those medications help with seizures as well as with anxiety.

The neurologist wanted me to stay in the hospital for four days to be continuously monitored on an EEG so that they could record the seizure when it happened. But because I was having problems with Medicaid, my insurance would not cover it. At least I had finally gotten an answer. The doctor was thinking about medicating me with Topamax, an antiseizure medicine, but I was already on Depakote, which was also an antiseizure medicine, and I'd had a severe reaction to Topamax many years before.

I decided to live with it and continue to take the anxiety medicine for it, as this usually calmed it down. Aside from this, everything was going well. I had a few students now to make a couple of dollars, and I was seeing both Geneva and Millie, plus I had dates with other women. Unfortunately, my eyes acted up during one of these dates, and it was very uncomfortable for me.

John and I had been living harmoniously together, but his collecting was getting out of control. The action figures were taking over the kitchen and the living room, and it just wasn't my thing. I like to set up my homes in a certain way, with beautiful art and religious items. I decided to call the leader of the apartment program to see if I could get my own place. She told me a small apartment had just become available in a very expensive building near the mall. I was familiar with the building because I had some friends who'd lived there for many years. I felt bad leaving John because he was such a cool guy and a good friend, but I really wanted my own space.

The new studio apartment was small, but I had it painted in my favorite color, which is blue, and I decorated it with beautiful artwork. It had a dishwasher and a small washer and dryer in a closet. I was ecstatic to have these things so conveniently located.

I was able to plug my guitar, keyboard, and microphones into my amplifiers and play there during normal hours and nobody ever complained. The woman next to me said that she loved music and that it wasn't a problem. I even heard the guy above me play his piano sometimes. I had two friends in the building, which made it cool as well. The mall was across the street, but I'm not much of a mall person, so I don't think I ever went there.

Like before, all around me were great places to eat. There was a delicious Italian restaurant, a deli for sandwiches, and Chinese and Mexican too. I was still driving the old Toyota, but it kept breaking down. Luckily my mom bought a new car for herself and gave me her 2013 Hyundai Sonata. I was so happy to be in a great car again. It had low miles and was in perfect condition. I knew it was a reliable car that I would have for years. In fact, that was eight years ago, and I still have it. I was busy settling into my life in the nice studio apartment by the mall and giving a few lessons for extra money, but I was not feeling well. I was tired all the time and did not know why.

I finally went to the doctor, who said he was sure I had sleep apnea. He wanted to send me for a sleep study, but my insurance made it difficult again. But at least I knew it wasn't something more serious, so I just lived with it.

Being back on Staten Island meant I could visit my mom and dad all the time. They were just a fifteen-minute drive away, and I liked to hang out with them. My father was suffering from early onset Alzheimer's, and it was very sad for me to watch him slowly disintegrate. It was also a huge burden for my mother, who was his primary caretaker. My mother had been through so much with me over the years, and now my dad was sick, and she had to take care of him full time too.

I was happy living in my new apartment and had been there less than a year when my mother decided to sell her house in Staten Island and move to a fifty-five and up community in New Jersey. This was very good news for me because my mom and I had a deal that we'd talked about many, many times over the years: when she was ready to sell the house, she would buy me a little house or condo upstate in the Catskills where I had always wanted to be.

This was like a dream come true for me now, and despite the fact that I would have to leave my friends and Geneva and Millie and the few students I had, I was so thrilled that my mountain dream would soon become a reality. I had even written about it in a third-grade assignment—how I would live in the Catskills in a little house with a fireplace, two dogs, three cats, and my wife and children and that there would be a lake in the back and I would live there forever. My mom found that story in the attic, and I still have it to this day.

My mom and I went to look at places in the Catskills that I had found online. She told me that she wanted me to rent for a year or two before she bought anything to make sure I liked it there. I knew I would, but I had to listen to her because it was her money. Eventually I found a place in Stone Ridge, New York, deep in the Catskills. It was a beautiful apartment in a woman's house that was modern and newly built. The backyard was simply forest that went back for miles and miles. The landlady told me not get lost back there because I would never find my way out.

I had to wait while my mom had her house cleaned out by a crew of people. She needed to get rid of forty years' worth of stuff to move into the small house in New Jersey. While I was waiting to move, I got a call one night from Geneva. Out of the blue, she said that she was moving to Brooklyn and that she was starting a new life and did not want to talk to me again. She wanted to meet that night and have sex one last time to say goodbye. She knew I was moving in a few months, but I thought that we'd at least stay in touch and visit sometimes. In a weird coincidence, Millie called at the same time I was talking to Geneva. Millie told me she was marrying her boyfriend and would never speak to me again because in a religious Jewish house, the wife could not have male friends. So, she too was calling to say goodbye.

I knew they were not my forever girls, but I did love them both and did not want them to leave my life completely and certainly not at the same time. It was devastating because I was now going to lose my two best friends and lovers all in one night. I ended up saying goodbye to Millie first while Geneva was on the other line. I was so mad at Geneva that I ended the conversation with a scream of "Fuck you!" I yelled it so loudly that I almost lost consciousness, and I literally saw stars and bright lights.

I had to say a lot of goodbyes before I moved to the Catskills. I said goodbye to my therapist, who I loved so much. She had done so much to help as I readjusted to normal life and assisted me with everyday problems. I had drawn her a sketch of a mermaid because I knew she loved them, and for our last appointment, I wrote a poem to honor her and our time together. She is really a very special human being, and I hope she still has the poem and the picture. At my last session, she gave me her email address and told me to keep in touch. I talked to her on the phone a couple of times, but we lost touch after that.

Saying goodbye to my students was difficult also. I talked to the mother of the autistic teenage boy on the phone, as they were in the process of moving, and I had not seen them for a few weeks. We were both very sad to say goodbye; I really loved the whole family.

Of my students, the hardest one to say goodbye to was a five-year-old girl I had been teaching for a while. I had found them a new piano teacher, but the grandma said the little girl was very upset that I was leaving. During the last lesson, I explained to her how I was moving upstate and would not see her again. After the lesson she stood by the piano, and I asked if she wanted to hug me goodbye. She ran across the room and jumped into my arms for a goodbye hug. It was probably the most adorable moment I'd ever had as a music teacher, and it makes me smile now to think about it.

Eventually the day came to move to Stone Ridge. I had my real piano with me, which had been in my parents' house all my life. Now I would be able to play it whenever I wanted. At my old house, the car was loaded up, and I said goodbye to my father and mother. My mom hugged me and cried and then I was off to my new life in upstate New York.

Chapter 23

LIVING IN STONE RIDGE, NEW YORK

(2016)

I moved into the new apartment, and it was really beautiful and secluded in the mountains. I had my piano back, and I set it up in the living room with all my old sheet music books that I had been collecting since I was a child. I put my guitar in the living room next to my piano, and I had a nice part of the room for a music studio. The only stipulation was that I could not play past 7:00 p.m. because the landlady liked to watch her TV programs at night.

    I got set up with an outpatient psych clinic, where I would get my therapy and injection and see a psychiatrist once a month to get my medicine. This was the most important thing. My social worker from Staten Island had found the place and had it all set up for me when I arrived. It was hard for them to find a permanent psychiatrist up there, so I had to see different ones. They kept me on my old protocol that had me stabilized for many years, so it was fine.

Once I got settled in, I decided to look for a job. I first went to a music school in Kingston, but they told me they had trouble finding students for the teachers they had. Apparently, it was not going to be as easy to find students in Ulster County as it was back home. I put my business cards on some bulletin boards, but it was a depressed economy and there were so few people there that I realized it was probably not going to happen.

I went instead to a place that tried to find jobs for disabled people. Unfortunately, my criminal record was a big problem for them, and even though we worked on a résumé, I never was able to find part-time employment. We got close with a job going to college classes with a physically disabled person and taking notes for them, but it did not pan out.

I loved the mountains and especially enjoyed watching the deer in the backyard or seeing them out front in the driveway. The landlady had two big black Labradors who were extremely friendly, but when I went in back to smoke a cigarette, they would jump all over me and each other trying to get attention. It was comical at times but sometimes annoying.

My insurance was fully working again, so I went to a sleep center and was tested for sleep apnea and other sleep disorders. They found I had severe sleep apnea and stopped breathing sixty times an hour while I slept. Now I knew for sure why I was always tired. The doctor prescribed me a CPAP machine to cure the problem, but for some reason I kept taking it off after an hour or two while I was sleeping. No matter how many times I put it on, I woke up with the mask on the floor.

My insurance stepped in and forced me to give back the machine for what they called noncompliance. This was absurd, as I put it on every single night and really wanted to get better, but the insurance company had a way of monitoring it through the onboard computer, and they took it away from me. Now I was stuck with severe sleep apnea and no real way to treat it. I could not drink coffee to help me because of my prior problems with rapid atrial fibrillation. The doctor had told me no caffeine at all. My solution was to sleep a lot, and sometimes I slept on the couch just for a change of scenery.

I liked to hang out in the backyard and watch the forest, but I didn't go on many hikes because I was afraid of Lyme disease, which is rampant there. I really did not know anybody and was completely alone, so I tried some things to meet people.

I started going to Friday night services at a progressive Jewish temple, and there I met a woman who had MS and who was very sweet and friendly. She was my age, and we became good friends. I hung out at her house a lot and got to know her family. She was divorced and had two sons and a dog, and she was very spiritual and into cool music. She was my first real friend after moving upstate. She lived in New Paltz in a nice house in the woods about a half hour away.

There was a really good pizzeria down the mountain, and the food was excellent. I ordered in from there a lot and went there often too. I became friendly with a pretty and cool woman in her thirties who worked there full time. She was very nice and kind to me, and although we never really hung out, I used to drop in there and chat with her all the time.

I was extremely isolated there, but I was not lonely. I was content to exist in the peace of the mountains and enjoy the Catskills, a place I had always dreamed about.

I got my haircuts in town from a young barber who worked with his mother. They were really nice and tried to help me find friends and network to try to find students. They also wanted me to play music for different places, but I had no plans to play shows again.

I went to an open mic night in New Paltz just to watch, and it was great to see all the people doing their music or poetry or even comedy acts. I recognized a couple of people from the old days, but I just said hello and moved on. The coffee shop in New Paltz was full, as the college kids and townspeople were all there to support the artists. It was different for me being in New Paltz as a sane and sober person. I did not feel the old pull to live there anymore.

I was overweight from the psych meds but not as heavy as I was when I was with Susan, so I thought I would go to a dietician to try to lose some weight and be healthier. I found a man online who lived in the area. I talked to him on the phone about what he did, and it sounded great. I made an appointment, but he called a few days later to cancel. He had an old client coming back and did not have the time for me. He said he could fit me in in about a month, but I was annoyed and asked him to recommend someone else.

He gave me the phone number of a young woman who lived far away. I called her and made an appointment. She was very nice. She lived on a farm like property in a private house with her boyfriend, and her parents and brother lived in others houses on the property. It turned out that I had known her brother from the old days. He ran a music shop in New Paltz.

Unfortunately, although she was a sweet and kindhearted person, she was not the best nutritionist, for me anyway. She tried to change my diet almost completely overnight, and I was just not ready for that. She wanted me to give up all white food, completely cutting out pizza, pasta, and rice. To do this at once would have been too difficult for me because Italian food is by far my favorite. Her other restrictions were going to be too severe for me as well. I saw her a couple of times and then went back to trying to eat in moderation. It was not like I was huge or anything, but I wanted to lose a few pounds. The meds made it difficult because they slowed down my metabolism and I was hungry a lot.

I started hanging out with Elizabeth, my friend with MS from New Paltz. One day she took me to a party at her friend's house in New Paltz. It was a lot of people our age, and they had all kinds of animals. The children took me into the house to see and play with the baby chicks, which was fun. There was also a basketball hoop, so I played some ball with some of the kids and adults. They ran an art gallery from their house as well as a small music venue, so these were very interesting people. They lived next to the nature preserve that I had slept in when I was homeless all those years ago. It was a great time, and we ended the night with a big bonfire and everybody sitting around the flames. I really do love bonfires.

On another occasion I went into New Paltz to see an art show and met the artists I had seen advertised somewhere. There were some really talented people there, and I got to talk to some of them. There was a lecture as well, and I asked some questions and joined in the discussion. I am not a trained artist in any way whatsoever, and I have never really taken an art lesson, but I do draw and paint sometimes as a hobby, though that was mostly when I was locked up in institutions.

I talked to an established artist who got her degree from the State University of New York at New Paltz. She told me that she'd been homeless for a year while she studied there and lived in her car. I asked if she could give me art lessons so that maybe I could actually know what I was doing. It was something I had always thought about because I do have some natural ability. She emailed me the number of someone in Woodstock who taught private lessons, but I never followed up with it. I did have a great time at the show that night, though.

Although things were going very well for me in Stone Ridge, the seizures in my eyes occurred more and more often, and it was getting pretty bad. I missed most of the Super Bowl because I literally could not focus on the television. I took some Klonopin and waited for it to pass, which it finally did.

I went to the Jewish services with Elizabeth sometimes, and it was a very different experience from what I was used to. The rabbi was a musician, and he played classical guitar and sang all these beautiful songs I had never heard of. I talked to him after the service about how the music was very spiritual. In addition, we had potluck dinners after the service to which everyone contributed. Because everything had to be vegetarian, I would bring guacamole and chips.

The landlady's kids would come around sometimes to visit and help her. The son was a corrections officer. He was a very kind man, and I would talk with him when I saw him. He came every time it snowed to plow the driveway and help his mom with splitting and putting away the firewood. She had a woodburning stove, and I loved the smell of the wood burning.

Every day I would drive down the mountain into the small town and get the newspapers, as I had done all my life in Staten Island. I never read the front of the paper because I hate the news; I bought them for the sports section. I have been following sports all my life and was happy that I could still get the *Daily News* and the *New York Post* all the way up there in Ulster County.

I opened a bank account at the Ulster County Savings Bank. They were very kind and gave me a gift of some battery-powered candles that I still have. Everybody was so nice in the mountains. It was such a slower pace than the city. People took their time and chatted with one another and were much more patient. I had spent most of my life in the city, so I really appreciated the gentleness and kindness of the people in the country.

After being in Stone Ridge for a while, I decided to try to quit smoking. I had smoked from nineteen to twenty-seven, then stopped when I had the irregular heartbeat. I started again when I was forty. I used over the counter nicotine patches and was able to stop for several years. It definitely helped my financial situation, and I hoped it would benefit my future health as well.

I went to the supermarket in town every week. I would buy my favorite foods and lots of bottles of orange Gatorade, which was my everyday drink. When it got dark, it was really dark, and even using my Garmin, I would still get lost sometimes coming back up the mountain to the apartment. Nighttime in the country is very different from in the city, and the roads were really dark. One time I drove into the woods by accident, but luckily, I was able to reverse my way out.

One day when I was driving to town, I saw a brown dachshund puppy in the middle of the street. I stopped the car on the winding country road and picked up the dog. I tried to see if its owner was around, but he had no leash, and I couldn't see anyone nearby. He was obviously lost, so I put him in the car and drove to town to see what I could do for him.

The poor puppy was exhausted and nervous and went to sleep on my lap. He was so cute, and I felt so badly for him that he had lost his owner. I first went into the pet store and bought him some food, but he was too nervous to eat. I then went to the supermarket, where I talked to the manager and an employee. They gave me the phone number of an animal rescue place. The man there said he would meet me at the store and take the dog to the shelter and try to find the owner on Facebook.

The animal rescue guy arrived pretty fast and took the dog to his car. The puppy was so adorable and sweet that I thought about taking him home with me, but I wanted the real owners to find him. I asked the rescue guy if they would put him to sleep if they couldn't find anyone, but he said, "Absolutely not." I felt the dog would be safe and hoped they'd find the owner or that he could be adopted by a new family. It was such a small town, they assured me that they would find the owner after they got the word out.

One day I was looking online at a spiritual bookstore in Woodstock when I saw a blurb about a healing circle led by a shaman. I knew both the shaman and his husband from New Jersey, and I knew they had moved to Saugerties after their store burned down in New Jersey. The bookstore was my favorite in the area. They offered frequent workshops and speakers, and the owner was a very sweet woman who was great to talk to.

At the healing circle, there were about six people and the shaman. I had nothing I was particularly looking to heal and was there just for the experience. We sat on chairs in a circle and put an object in the center near a few holy objects the shaman had put out. Then he smudged the room and us with sage and began the ceremony. We closed our eyes, and the shaman sang and danced and drummed, and we all took in the good vibes.

The whole thing cost me like a five-dollar donation, but here is the great part. I never had a seizure again. That was seven years ago, and

I have not had any problems with my eyes since. Epilepsy had tortured me on and off for twenty years, and in one almost-hour session with this man, it has never returned. If you think this kind of stuff is just new age quackery, I am proof that it can and does work. Our ancestors may not have had technology, but they were not stupid people at all.

My time in Stone Ridge was coming to an end. My landlady wanted me to move out and told me some story about having to sell the house. I knew she was making it up because I saw the apartment for rent online. She and I had never had the warmest of relationships, and she had mental problems of her own.

I started looking for apartments in different areas, especially Woodstock, as it was such a fun place and had that 1960s vibe I loved. I looked at an apartment there, but it did not suit me. Then, quite by accident, I pulled into a street with some blue houses in the woods. I got out to look around and a tall young man asked if I was looking for the apartment for rent. I thought this was quite serendipitous and told him I would check it out.

He took me up a long narrow flight of stairs in the back of one of the houses and showed me a three-hundred-square-foot apartment with a tiny old bathroom and a very small kitchen. It was dimly lit, but I knew with my two cats, I would have a lot of trouble finding a place that allowed pets, and Woodstock is a very expensive place to live.

I liked that the house was right off the main street, so I would not be so isolated anymore and could walk into town if I wanted to. Plus, it was set back from the road with a stream and a nature preserve behind it. The size was not a problem, as I've always liked small places and it made me feel cozy. I also liked that it was an attic apartment and had a tilted roof, which I thought was cool.

I got the landlord's number, and we agreed on a price and a year lease. He also agreed to let me have the cats, which was essential for me. My mom would pay the rent, as there was no way I could afford it on my disability check. The landlord called a few references I gave him, and I moved in at the beginning of the month.

Chapter 24

LIVING IN WOODSTOCK, NEW YORK

(2017-2021)

Woodstock was an awesome experience for me and a great place to live. I fixed up the apartment with my tie-dye sheet hanging from one wall and lots of beautiful artwork and religious items. I prominently displayed my hand-carved wooden Buddha statue I had gotten in New Paltz many years before. My piano and couch would never have fit in the small space, so I put them in a temperature-controlled storage facility so that my piano would not be destroyed. I put a bunch of other things in storage as well and was very happy to move into the historic town.

I became friends with the couple who lived beneath me. Aron and Heather were really cool people and had lived there for many years. He was a writer for the local newspaper, and she worked at a local hotel. They were artsy people and loved animals, so we had a lot in common.

We went out together to an open mic night down the block and had a lot of fun. Aron and Heather became my closest friends upstate, and we had so many great times and conversations. They did not care if I played my music through amplifiers and microphones, so I could sing to my heart's content during normal hours. In fact, Heather would encourage me to sing a lot as she really enjoyed my songs. Aron was a musician too but had a lot of problems with his eyes; I think he played more when he was younger. They were both a bit older than me.

We had a party for the three of us on Super Bowl Sunday. Heather made her famous guacamole for the event, and it was amazing. We hung out a lot and were always there for one another to feed the others' cats or provide whatever help was needed. I always felt safe and secure knowing they were right beneath me.

Because I lived off the main street, everything was really convenient for me. There was a CVS right down the street where I could get my medications and newspapers and lots of groceries too. The assistant manager there was a girl in her late twenties who I found really beautiful and supersmart. I talked to her all the time, and we had some great conversations. She became my Woodstock crush. She had a longtime boyfriend, so I never asked her out, but I always enjoyed talking to her.

She was looking for a job in the music industry, like working for a record company, and was disappointed that she did not have any luck finding one. She had a master's degree, and I would try to help her by giving her suggestions and rooting for her to fulfill her dreams. She told me she did not want to be famous but instead wanted to help other people get famous. She was a ski instructor in her spare time and really enjoyed outdoor activities.

I found all my usual food places down the block, including a real deli for sandwiches. In addition, there was a health food store that had lots of prepared meals and other stuff I liked.

One of the cool things about Woodstock was that a lot of celebrities had country homes there, and I would spot a famous actress or actor every once in a while. The stores all had a cool hippie or artistic vibe, and it was always fun to go window-shopping and check out the funky boutiques.

One night Aron, Heather, and I and their niece built a fire in a firepit and hung out until very late. Heather and Aron drank their wine, and their niece smoked her pot. I had my cigarettes, which I had started smoking again. Heather and Aron smoked cigarettes as well. The stars were out, and the fire smelled so wonderful. It was a perfect Woodstock evening. We talked long into the night.

My heater was broken, and the propane company wanted $1,500 to put in a new tank, so I made the best of it and bought a space heater. The apartment was so small that it easily heated the whole place, even on the coldest of nights. I could not use my stove, but I had a microwave, a toaster oven, and an electric frying pan. I made do, and it did not bother me at all. I ordered in a lot too.

The holidays were awesome in Woodstock as well. On Christmas there was a huge parade in the evening that everybody came out to watch. They had bands, and Santa would come into the parade in a different cool way every year. One time he came down the street in a cherry picker truck, and I heard he parachuted in another time. Everybody would walk around the lit-up streets and have a great time. It was a really beautiful celebration.

Halloween was even more fun because the stores along the main street opened their doors for the children and gave out tons of delicious candy. The employees dressed up in amazing costumes and really put their hearts into it. Lots of other people dressed up too, and there was a great scene of people all day.

My life was peaceful and happy. I felt at home, and I knew I truly wanted to live my life in Ulster County. I spent time playing my guitar or keyboard and singing or hanging out with Heather and Aron. I read a lot and enjoyed listening to music more than ever before. I spent hours and hours every day listening to YouTube, where I discovered so many of my now favorite artists.

I enjoyed just hanging out with my two cats who were so sweet and fun. I had everything I wanted and was content. I did not have a girlfriend, but I really did not care. I found such peace and harmony living in those mountains and figured I would meet the right girl eventually.

I did date a little while I was there. There was one Filipino girl I really liked, and we went out a few times. She was cute and smart and was an occupational therapist. Just when we were starting to hit it off, her company transferred her to another city way upstate, so that never had a chance to really blossom. I took it in stride and figured I would meet somebody cool in the future.

After living in Woodstock for a while, I got the call from my mother in Florida that I knew was going to come eventually. My father had died from Alzheimer's disease after a fifteen-year battle. I was sad, but he had deteriorated so much over the years that I was glad he was no longer suffering.

The last time I had been with him had been at my parents' house in New Jersey, and he had been all bent over in his wheelchair and was shaking from Parkinson's disease as well. It really tore me up. While sitting at the dinner table, I broke down and cried hysterically. To see my dad who I loved so much in that state was more than I could bear.

My mother told me to make arrangements, so I had a neighbor watch and feed my cats, and I made the two-hour drive from Woodstock to Monroe Township in New Jersey. The funeral was sad, but knowing he was no longer suffering was a great relief for myself and my family. My mother had watched the man she loved slowly get sick and leave his senses over the years. She had been his primary caretaker. For the last three years of his life, she'd hired a nurse, an extremely kind Filipino man, to be with them twenty-four hours a day, seven days a week.

After the funeral and the traditional Jewish shiva, I came back to Woodstock and went back to leading my life of peace and tranquility. I really did not grieve after that because I had already lost the man I knew as my strong, wonderful father many years before. The next night after I returned, my father came to me in a dream and told me to clean up my room. My small studio apartment was kind of a big mess at that point, so I was comforted by his spirit visiting me to advise me one last time. I knew that he was in heaven and that his soul was finally at rest.

While I was living in the beautiful Catskills, the COVID-19 pandemic hit the world and everything changed. We were on lockdown and could go out only for essential services. Everybody wore masks, and there was a great fear among everyone. I did not watch any news or much TV at all and did not read the news, so I was even more isolated than before.

However, instead of becoming lonely or depressed, I loved it. COVID-19 was and is a terrible illness, and I know that millions of people have died from it or have had their lives turned upside down. But for me, it was one of the most peaceful and happy times of my life. I loved being a hermit and I loved the solitude. It was so peaceful to just be. I grew closer to God and prayed every day. It was a simple life, and I was free of any kind of responsibility, as my mom paid my rent, and I had my disability check for food and essentials. I was poor but happy. My car worked fine, and I had enough to eat. This simple and quiet solitude was probably the happiest time of my life.

The telephone was my major source of socialization during the pandemic. I talked to my mom every day and to my cousin Elijah about once a week. Elijah was the son of my godmother and great-aunt who died right around my wedding. He and I had worked on different projects together over the years. He's a brilliant man and is a professional videographer and photographer.

Elijah was great to talk to, as we have so much in common. He's more than twenty years older than me and had been at the original

Woodstock in 1969. We shared so many of the same passions, including music, art, philosophy, and spirituality. He was someone I could talk to on a high intellectual level, and I loved our conversations. He is a musician as well and had been in a band in the sixties.

I also talked to Abe, who was still living in Staten Island, and a few other friends from back home. But mostly I was alone. I can't describe how beautiful solitude can be. I loved it. I had always longed for peace. My life had been so turbulent and crazy, but now I had found the peace in my heart and soul that I so desired.

There were certain things I had to go out for, of course, like food, picking up my medication, and getting my injection of Prolixin every three weeks for my mental illness. But now everything was happening virtually, so I would talk to my therapist on the phone and only go out for the essentials.

While living in Woodstock, I spent many hours simply thinking. I was content to just lie in my bed and think. I would go into something I called the zone. This was where my mind would get incredibly quiet and my whole being would be at peace. I don't know if you'd call it meditation or contemplation or what, but I did it every day, and it was a beautiful feeling.

I started to read all the sports sections I love online instead of buying newspapers every day like I had done for years. I subscribed to the sports section online, and it was much cheaper in the long run, as the New York City papers were much more expensive upstate. I also subscribed to *The Athletic*, which is an online sports magazine. This also helped me keep the apartment clean because it did not pile up with papers that needed to be recycled. I liked to eat my meals and read the sports, something I'd done all my life when I was alone.

I did not watch much television anymore, but sometimes I would watch old sitcoms in the middle of the night like *The King of Queens* or *Mom*. I love to laugh, and comedy is my favorite kind of entertainment after music. I don't like violence of any kind and won't watch anything that contains it. Even the news on TV is so triggering for me that I never watch it because it can give me nightmares. I don't know how people who watch it every night then sleep after. I am an extremely gentle person, so I am too sensitive to watch that kind of thing. Especially given all the violence I had experienced in my life; you can understand why I detest it so much.

My favorite place to go in Woodstock was always the bookstore. Even when I lived on Staten Island, bookstores were my favorite places to frequent. I would go all the time to the big Barnes and Noble on Richmond Avenue and browse and read and write for hours. My love affair with books will never end. I cherish them. I hardly ever read novels, as I prefer nonfiction. I want to learn something from every book I read. The loss of my library of books after my last manic episode still bothers me to this day. Those books were part of my life and represented different eras and what I was learning at the time. I just hope they are making some people happy who are lucky enough to read them. It took me forty years to collect them.

Even though I've always loved nature and watching the trees and wildlife, I did not do much of that in Woodstock. This was partly due to my fear of Lyme disease, but mostly I just felt content to be in my tiny apartment. It was really kind of a crappy place in a one-hundred-plus-year-old attic, but it was home. I had grown content beyond anything I'd ever experienced before. My life was happy at last.

After three years of living in Woodstock and loving upstate New York, my mother fully intended to make good on her decades-old promise to buy me a small house or condo in Ulster County. I started to look at real estate listings and talk to real estate agents in the search for my dream home.

The problem was that the pandemic had changed everything. People were leaving the city in droves, and the cost of housing skyrocketed. It was a huge sellers' market. The final blow was that there were so many people wanting to move upstate that the sellers would not even let me do a home inspection to see if the house was in good condition. My mother and I would not tolerate this, as you would never know what you would be getting. It was too risky.

I came home to my mom's house in New Jersey, and we talked about what we were going to do. Mom wanted me out of that apartment because she thought it was a piece of shit and did not want me living there. I kind of thought I should move on as well, but I wanted to finally own something where I could live forever.

One day when I was in my dad's old room, I had what I can only describe as an intuition. I felt a sensation move through my body from my head to my toes. It came to me that I should move into my mom's house. It was a weird thought because I loved it upstate, and it had always been my dream to be there. My mom lived in the house for only five months out of the year and stayed in Boca Raton, Florida, the rest of the time. I loved living alone and had no desire to move in with my mother again, but for some reason I felt like this was what God wanted me to do.

I discussed the idea with my mom, and she thought it was a fantastic solution. The beautiful house was nineteen hundred square feet with two bedrooms and two bathrooms in a fifty-five and over community. Even though I was only fifty-one at the time, the rules of the community stated that if a fifty-five or older person owned the house, someone could live there who was forty-eight or older. My mom was happy I could take care of her as she got older and watch the house when she was gone. I agreed somewhat reluctantly because my dream had always been to live upstate, even though I had always liked New Jersey.

After three years and three months in Woodstock, I moved into my mother's house in Monroe Township, New Jersey. I had my own beautiful room with the walls painted my favorite color blue. I had a real bathroom with tiles and a tub, and everything was new and beautiful. My mother even told me I could make part of the big open concept dining room my music studio. I got my piano back and set up my office and computer and moved in.

Chapter 25

LIVING IN MONROE TOWNSHIP, NEW JERSEY

(2021 – Present)

In New Jersey, I found an outpatient clinic and a nurse practitioner who could give my injection every three weeks and prescribe my medication. Judy is a wonderful woman whose office is about thirty minutes away. She is very conscientious and helpful to me. She is great to talk to and is extremely dedicated to and serious about my mental health. There was even an occasion when she was very sick and came in just to give me the injection because she knew how important it is to my sanity.

I had to do all the normal things one does when you move, and so I had my car registered and insured in New Jersey and got a New Jersey driver's license. I found a doctor who could give me my cholesterol and prediabetes medications. He is a very nice Indian man whose office is only five minutes away.

My cats, Boris and Linus, are much happier in a bigger house instead of being confined in that little apartment in Woodstock. They purr a lot more, and Linus has stopped trying to get out all the time like he did in Woodstock.

Everything is so convenient to where I now live. There is a Stop and Shop down the block, a great pizzeria, Chinese and Mexican food, an Indian restaurant, and a diner all within a five-minute drive of my house. CVS and my pharmacy are nearby as well, so it was easy to settle into my neighborhood.

The town itself is beautiful, with trees and fields and lots of open spaces. The gated community where I live is beautiful too, almost like a park. The backyard is small but perfectly situated in a green space. I love to smoke my cigarettes out there and enjoy nature and the birds and small cute bunnies and chipmunks and squirrels.

I am in the suburbs now, and I am enjoying it a lot. It's a great neighborhood, and people are very friendly and polite in the stores. Some of the Jersey drivers can be a little aggressive because I always do the speed limit, as I don't want any police involvement. My cousin is a police officer nearby here.

The best part of living in Monroe Township is being close to my family. I can see my sisters and brother-in-law and nephews and nieces on the holidays, which means a lot to me. My cousin Elijah lived not too far away, although he now lives in Florida, and my longtime friend Jenn, who is a great artist, lives about thirty minutes from me.

I have been friends with Jenn for about twenty-five years. We initially met on a dating site but became good friends instead. Jenn is a remarkable talent and creates realistic paintings. She also does caricatures at occasions, and her artwork has been in famous galleries in Manhattan and elsewhere. She has been written up in magazines was well.

She is very important to me because she has remained friends with me through thick and thin. She saw everything happen during my meltdown and beyond and still kept in touch with me, even after most of my other friends were afraid to. She is a busy person, but we get together for dinner when we can. It's nice to have her so close by. We share a love of art, music, and animals. Jenn is one of the most brilliant people I have ever met, and I love talking to her.

When I first moved back, I got a call from a woman named Peggy, who I had met on a dating site and hooked up with before I moved upstate. She grew up in Staten Island and is a few years younger than me. She had lived only a few blocks away in my old neighborhood. She now lives only an exit down the turnpike from my house.

When I was upstate, we had kept in touch for a while but eventually stopped talking. It was a remarkable timing when she called me only a little while after I had moved to New Jersey, so near to her. She came over one night, and we hooked up again and had a great time. She came over a little bit after this, and we fooled around again, but I only wanted to be platonic friends. I just did not think we were compatible beyond that. She wanted more out of the relationship, so unfortunately, we have not kept in touch that often.

My mom got a dog from a rescue organization after her cat died from a long battle with cancer. The dog had been abused and been part of a puppy mill. She was found starving on the streets, and after my mom adopted her, she needed to be spayed and have a hernia operation. Riley Anne, which my mom named her, has a lot of special needs. She has separation anxiety and will cry and howl anytime my mother leaves her alone. She also is food aggressive and can get mean if you get too close to her food. Riley is a small dog, about eighteen pounds, and some kind of terrier. She is cute and loves me too, but my mom is by far her first love and support system. She was supposed to be an emotional support dog for mom, but I think it's the other way around.

My cats and Riley don't get along very well, and I need to keep them separated. This has worked out okay, as I have a different schedule from my mother. I usually go to bed around dawn and sleep into the afternoon. I've had this reverse sleep cycle since I was young, and it was the major reason I hated school until college. When my mother goes to sleep at about ten o'clock, I let the cats out so that they can roam the house all night. When I go to sleep in the morning, I take them into my room and close the door.

Our two schedules work very well together, and Mom and I get along better than we ever have. Boris is always good and never causes a fuss, but Linus is such a scamp and will wake me up a lot by sticking his paw in my ear so that I'll give him treats a few times during the night. It's annoying, but I can never be mad at him very long, as he is such a sweet cat.

There are many advantages to living in New Jersey that I did not have upstate. One is that I am closer to my friends on Staten Island, so I can visit them from time to time. My best friend, Dell, lives in the city and works in finance, but he is frequently in Staten Island to visit his parents. Dell and I have been friends for thirty-five years. I met him through a high school friend, and we have been through so much together.

Dell is extremely intelligent and very, very funny. It's humor that has kept us close throughout the years. He is my oldest fried who I have been consistently in touch with my whole adult life. Unlike so many of my other close friends, he never left me through all my nervous breakdowns and troubles. His father is Saudi Arabian, and his mom is Irish, so a lot of our humor together is based on our Arab/Jewish relationship. He is a republican and I lean heavily toward the left, but we never argue. We just make jokes about each other and have fun. He is the only friend I talked to when I was in Rikers Island.

Dell works in finance, but his dream is to be a screenwriter; he writes comedy scripts. He has a master's degree in film, and he hates the nine-to-five. I hope that someday he will get his scripts made into movies. We talk every Sunday after he comes home from church, and I look forward to the conversation all week. We love to crack each other up, although we do talk seriously a lot as well. Dell is a very spiritual person, so we have that in common too.

One of the best parts of living with my mom again after all these years is her cooking. She is a fantastic cook, and everything she makes is amazing. When she is in Florida, I mostly eat frozen food or takeout. When she is home, I get to have real home-cooked dinners again. Her matzo ball soup is amazing, as is her stir-fry, meatloaf, and sloppy joes. She cooks a lot of vegetables, and like any mom, she is always trying to encourage me to eat healthy.

What I found here in New Jersey mostly is peace. I have such a peaceful life, even more than in Woodstock. I spend a lot of time praying and growing closer to God. I read more, and the best thing about it is that I have my original piano back after so many years. And I can play all night while my mother is in Florida and most times until she goes to sleep when she is here. The houses are very well built in this development, and the neighbors said that they don't hear me play or sing at all. So, I have all night to play music.

I got my piano tuned and fixed, as there were two broken notes for fifteen years, and now it is like a revelation. I love playing my piano again and have gotten much more into my music. I bought for myself an expensive Martin DM-28 guitar using the stimulus money I had saved. It was the fulfillment of a dream to have a guitar of that quality and beauty. Even though I mostly play classical guitar, I have always wanted to write songs and play my strumming songs on a steel string, so I was very happy with this purchase.

This is a retirement community, although some residents do go to work. There is a clubhouse with an indoor and outdoor pool and a library. There is a small theater for shows and a big room filled with nice tables where the women play mah-jongg or canasta. There is a gym too, and outside of the clubhouse are tennis courts and pickleball courts.

All of these things are cool but not really for me. I have been in the clubhouse only twice and don't use any of the facilities. I am just a happy hermit living a sweet, peaceful life in my house. I don't leave the house very often and mostly just stay in my room and enjoy my peaceful life.

I do like to go in the backyard and sit in my chair and smoke cigarettes and pray to God. I am so grateful for everything I have and for all that God and my mom have given me. I love the parklike outdoors in this community. I see bunnies and deer and all kinds of animals, and the birds are always singing in the nice weather. My favorites are what I call the morning birds because they start singing every day at around 4:00 a.m. I love to listen to them, as they seem so happy in their songs.

My cousin Elijah and I have gotten very close since I moved here, and I talk to him on the telephone all the time. My mother and I went to a commemorative luncheon for Elijah's first wife, who died from liver failure much too young. I had not seen her since their son's wedding, but she was an important person to me when I was growing up, so I wanted to attend. She was very into angels. Her angel collection was on all the tables, and they told us to take them home. I took three little angel statues that are on my bookcase now. I have always believed in angels, and I think I have seen them on a few occasions. I know that they work in all our lives and that every person on Earth has a guardian angel.

I read a lot, mostly spiritual books, but I like memoirs and biographies too. I read the Steve Jobs biography and really liked it. I have always been a huge fan of Apple products, and that is all I use. There is something just beautiful about all Apple products besides the technology, and I know that was important to Mr. Jobs.

Before I started writing this book, I made sure to read a bunch of modern memoirs to get a feel for how they are written. I never took any writing courses, so I learned from the memoirs themselves. But I have been writing since childhood, from poetry to stories to books when I got older, but this is my first memoir that I am going to try to get it into people's hands.

The other great friend I have in Staten Island is Tom, who is a Grammy Award-winning engineer and also a producer. He has an amazing studio in his house near the mall, and I love being there with him.

We made an album about fourteen years ago, and it was a lot of fun. He knew I was mentally ill when we recorded that album, but he continued to stick by me anyway. He helped me when I was homeless by giving me food and clothing.

When I got better, we started to build a real friendship, and now I consider him one of my closest friends. Tom is a musical genius and a very kind, sensitive soul. He is very close to God and has been through a lot. We have plans to make another album in the summer.

I am still very close to my friend Abe, who lives in Staten Island, and we talk almost every day. Abe is still in the apartment program that I was in, but now he is working full time.

The thing I do the most of here in Monroe Township is listen to music. I have such a love of music, and it brings out all the emotions in my soul. I subscribed to YouTube Premium so that I don't get advertisements, and I bought the big Apple headphones. On average, I listen to music about six hours a day. Music was not available when I was homeless or locked up, which added to my suffering.

One thing I did when I was homeless was take some cheap headphones into the library and listen to music on their computers. At that time my favorite was Avril Lavigne, specifically her album *Goodbye Lullaby*. I would watch those videos on YouTube again and again, and it made me happy. Even when I got better, I still loved her music; it got me through so many hard times. I have listened to that album, mostly tracks four and thirteen, thousands of times, and I never get bored of it. There is just something magical about that woman and her music.

I was diagnosed with prediabetes when I lived in Stone Ridge, and they had put me on diabetes medication. I was also taking a statin for high cholesterol as well as my usual mental health medication. I found a really good endocrinologist through my nurse practitioner, and she took blood work and tried to put me on one of the new weight loss medications. Unfortunately, my insurance would not cover it. I was upset because I was still overweight from the psych meds, and I really hated not being fit.

I went back to her a few months later for more blood work. I was now fully diabetic, according to my A1C levels, and she was able to put me on Ozempic, which is for diabetes and is also a weight loss drug. My insurance covered it, even though it was still hundreds of dollars every three months. Luckily my mom came through yet again and helped me pay for it.

I was not happy to be diabetic, but I was excited by the prospect of finally losing weight after all these years of being heavy due to psych meds. Whenever I was off those medications, I had been skinny. I am naturally a thin person, and the mental health medications made me constantly hungry and slowed down my metabolism. I just had to accept my fate that I would always be fat if I wanted to be sane.

Now with this new miracle medication, I knew I would possibly be able to lose a lot of weight. I started on a small dose and lost two and a half pounds the first week. After that it was very slow. I would lose a pound here and there and sometimes not at all or even gain back a pound. Eventually the doctor increased the Ozempic to 2 milligrams, and I started to lose weight more frequently as the weeks and months went by. The main side effects are nausea for the first couple of days after the injection and sometimes an upset stomach. Still, it is nothing compared to the joy I feel in actually losing weight.

As I write this, I have lost twenty-five pounds and can fit into some of my old jeans. My stomach is basically flat, and I have lost my double chin so that you can see the bone structure in my face again. I am so happy. I really have no words to describe it. I never thought I could be a thin person again. I still want to lose another fifteen pounds, but it is not easy. I watch everything I eat and don't order out all the time like I was doing, but it is so worth it. I don't have the appetite that I've had for my whole adult life taking the meds. I feel so much more confident now and can look in the mirror again and be content. I thank God for Ozempic. It has really changed my life.

The last time I went to my endocrinologist, my diabetes level was perfect, as was my cholesterol level. I am completely healthy. There was a point years ago when my triglyceride level was over 3000, and it is supposed to be lower than 150, so I was at a high risk for a heart attack or stroke. Now my triglyceride levels are down to only 200, and I know they will be normal when I lose more weight. This has made me so happy.

Here is where my story comes to an end. I have taken you through many years of my life and showed you what it was like to live with a mental illness for my whole adult life. My life has been extremely difficult yet also filled with wonderful people and great times. I do think my life is a story of hope. I have been stable and happy for the last ten years and have been able to live a semi normal life. I hope that I can inspire you to never give up. I do believe that through faith in God and a little courage, you can get through anything.

I went through drug and alcohol addiction problems when I was younger, as you read, and I was extremely mentally ill for many periods of my life and suffered greatly. My parents and family suffered too, as they had to witness and experience my problems with me.

In writing this book, I hope to help people persevere and gain faith so that they can get through their mental health issues. Bipolar disorder is a really bad disease, and I would not wish it on my worst enemy. If you are suffering from it or from other mental health problems, I implore you not to kill yourself or to give up trying to get better. Today's medications can really turn your life around, so never, ever give up.

EPILOGUE

God does not waste anyone's lifetime. We are all here for a reason—we are here to learn and to love and to forgive. I do believe the only way to achieve peace in our hearts and in the world at large is through radical forgiveness. Love and forgiveness are the only path. I have been harmed by many people, as you have read in this book, some even trying to kill me or beat me senseless. It takes strength to forgive completely. I don't claim to have yet achieved complete forgiveness in my heart, but I am trying.

I have harmed others as well, mostly during my manic episodes and drunken behavior. I hope these people can find it in their hearts, minds, and souls to forgive me one day. I certainly never wanted to hurt anyone, and I regret many of the consequences of my actions throughout my lifetime.

Luckily, I have found peace in my mind and soul over the last ten years, and a lot of that has been due to the doctors finding the right medications to keep me stable. It does not mean I am perfect. I still have plenty of anxiety and ups and downs like most people.

It is also important that I remain sober and drug-free so that I can lead a high quality of life and make good decisions. I have learned so much, and I thank God for giving me life; I hope I stay sane and sober for the rest of it. There are no guarantees, though, as you all must realize. This is the Earth school, so anything can happen. Being human is a very difficult job, and nobody goes through life unscathed.

That is the way it was meant to be, though. When we are in heaven and between lives, there is no suffering and there is no pain; there is nothing but bliss. That is our true home and our real existence. God created us to be happy and eternal beings. He gave us souls that are in his image, and he wants his children to be happy and wise.

He sent us here to the Earth school to be educated and learn and to become better souls. He did this the same way we send our children here to school to be educated and to become socialized and better human beings. The Earth is not our only reality; it is simply a temporary condition. We are born, we live, we learn, we love, we suffer, we get old, we die. This is our shared experience on Earth.

We all are brothers and sisters together. Please do not hate anyone, as we are in reality all one family. War and violence and hatred are simply things that are fostered by the illusion that we are somehow different from one another because we have different-colored skin or different religions or different ethnicities. We are all God's children, and he loves us all equally. When you look into someone's eyes, try to see that spark of God that is their soul looking back at you.

We all want the same things in life no matter who we are or where we live. Every person wants a warm shelter, good food, family, love, friendship, health, and peace. God wants this for us too, but we all must work together as his children to achieve this for one another. We have been making it more difficult for ourselves with the hatred.

My life as a person with bipolar disorder has been terrible at some points and amazingly beautiful at others. I think everyone can probably say that if they live long enough, but I can only tell you my story; you have your own story to live. I wish you peace and serenity.

God bless you all.

www.davidwilliamweisner.net

www.ingramcontent.com/pod-product-compliance
Lightning Source LLC
Chambersburg PA
CBHW050223100526
44585CB00017BA/1873